Interactions Among Living Things

HOUGHTON MIFFLIN

BOSTON

You Can...

Do What Scientists Do

Meet Dr. Dale Brown Emeagwali. She works as a teacher and researcher at Morgan State University in Baltimore, Maryland. Dr. Emeagwali is a microbiologist, which is a biologist who specializes in studying single-celled organisms, or microorganisms. The goal of her investigations is to gain a better understanding of the processes that take place inside cells. Depending on the question she is investigating, Dr. Emeagwali may observe these living things in nature or conduct an experiment in the laboratory.

Scientists ask questions. Then they answer the questions by investigating and experimenting. Dr. Emeagwali has asked many questions about how microorganisms carry out their life processes, as well as how they affect human health.

In one investigation, she demonstrated that a certain chemical exists in a type of bacteria called *Streptomyces parvulus.* Such discoveries add to the basic knowledge of microbiology. Dr. Emeagwali is pleased, though, when her work has practical applications in medicine. In another experiment, she demonstrated that certain molecules could be used to stop the formation of tumors in people with cancer.

Dr. Emeagwali understands that for each investigation she carries out she must repeat the procedure many times and get the same results before she can conclude that her results are true.

Science investigations involve communicating with other scientists.

In addition to laboratory research, Dr. Emeagwali spends time writing papers about her work in order to communicate with other scientists. She wants other scientists to be able to repeat her investigations in order to check that her results are valid. Dr. Emeagwali also spends time reading about the work of other scientists to keep informed about the progress others have made in microbiology.

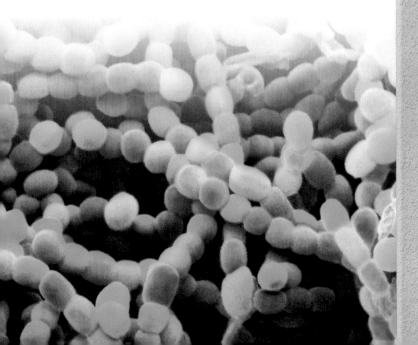

Think Like a Scientist

The ways scientists ask and answer questions about the world around them is called **scientific inquiry.** Scientific inquiry requires certain attitudes, or approaches to thinking about a problem. To think like a scientist you have to be:

- curious and ask a lot of questions.

- creative and think up new ways to do things.

- able to keep an open mind. That means you consider the ideas of others.

- willing to use measurement, estimation, and other mathematics skills.

- open to changing what you think when your investigation results surprise you.

- willing to question what other people tell you.

What kind of rock is this? How did this rock form? Where did the different materials that make up the rock come from?

Use Critical Thinking

When you think critically, you make decisions about what others tell you or what you read. Is what you heard on TV or read in a magazine a fact or an opinion? A *fact* can be checked to make sure it is true. An *opinion* is what someone thinks about the facts.

Did you ever hear a scientific claim that was hard to believe? When you think, "What evidence is there to support that claim?" you are thinking critically. You'll also think critically when you evaluate investigation results. Observations can be interpreted in many ways. You'll judge whether a conclusion is supported by the data collected.

The book states that a sedimentary rock forms when rock fragments and other sediments are pressed and cemented together.

It looks like fragments of different kinds of rock came together to make this rock. This must be a type of sedimentary rock.

Science Inquiry

Applying scientific inquiry helps you understand the world around you. Suppose you have decided to investigate which color is easiest to see clearly in the dimmest light.

Observe In the evening, as daylight fades, you observe the different colored objects around you. As the light becomes dimmer and dimmer, you notice which color remains clear to your eyes.

Ask a Question When you think about what you saw, heard, or read, you may have questions.

Hypothesis Think about facts you already know. Do you have an idea about the answer? Write it down. That is your *hypothesis*.

Experiment Plan a test that will tell if the hypothesis is true or not. List the materials you will need. Write the steps you will follow. Make sure that you keep all conditions the same except the one you are testing. That condition is called the *variable*.

Conclusion Think about your results. What do they tell you? Did your results support your hypothesis or show it to be false?

Describe your experiment to others. Communicate your results and conclusion.

My Color Experiment

Observe As the light dims, dark colors such as dark blue seem to disappear from sight first.

Ask a question I wonder which color can be seen most clearly in the dimmest light?

Hypothesis Yellow is the color that can be seen most clearly in the dimmest light.

Experiment I'm going to observe several differently colored objects as I dim the light. Then I'm going to observe which color I can see most clearly in the dimmest light.

Conclusion The results support my hypothesis. Yellow is the color that can be seen most clearly in the dimmest light.

Inquiry Process

The methods of science may vary from one area of science to another. Here is a process that some scientists follow to answer questions and make new discoveries.

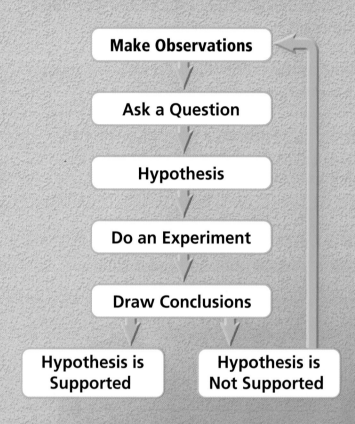

Make Observations

Ask a Question

Hypothesis

Do an Experiment

Draw Conclusions

Hypothesis is Supported

Hypothesis is Not Supported

Science Inquiry Skills

You'll use many of these skills of inquiry when you investigate and experiment.

- Ask Questions
- Observe
- Compare
- Classify
- Predict
- Measure

- Hypothesize
- Use Variables
- Experiment
- Use Models
- Communicate
- Use Numbers

- Record Data
- Analyze Data
- Infer
- Collaborate
- Research

Try It Yourself!

Experiment With Energy Beads

When you hold Energy Beads in your fist for a while and then go outdoors and open your hand, the beads change from off-white to many different colors.

1 What questions do you have about the Energy Beads?

2 How would you find out the answers?

3 How could you use Energy Beads to test a hypothesis?

4 Write your plan for an experiment with one variable using Energy Beads. Predict what will happen.

Be an Inventor

Cassandra "Cassie" Wagner became an inventor when she was 11 years old. At that time, she was in middle school. During the summer, she wanted to make a toy for her pet cat. Cats are attracted to catnip, a plant with a strong odor. Cassie considered including catnip as part of her toy.

When Cassie researched about catnip on the Internet, she discovered that some people thought an oil in the plant will repel insects. She could find no proof of that hypothesis, and so she decided to test it herself. In her first experiment, Cassie put a small amount of the oil from catnip onto a cotton ball. She then observed whether mosquitoes were repelled by the ball. They were.

With the help of a University of Florida professor, Cassie ran further experiments in a laboratory. She proved that the spray she made with the catnip oil repelled insects just as well as bug sprays sold in stores.

Cassie called her bug repellent Bugnip, and she planned to have it produced and sold to consumers. In the future, her efforts may lead to other inventions and better ways of repelling bothersome bugs.

"It was over the summer, and I didn't have much going on. I was just fooling around."

What Is Technology?

The tools people make and use, the things they build with tools, and the methods used to accomplish a practical purpose are all technology. A toy train set is an example of technology. So is a light rail system that provides transportation in a major city.

Scientists use technology, too. For example, a telescope makes it possible for scientists to see objects far into space that cannot be seen with just the eyes. Scientists also use measurement technology to make their observations more exact.

Many technologies make the world a better place to live. Sometimes, though, a technology that solves one problem can cause other problems. For example, burning coal in power plants provides power for generators that produce electricity for homes, schools, and industries. However, the burning of coal also can cause acid rain, which can be very harmful to living things.

A Better Idea

"I wish I had a better way to _____." How would you fill in the blank? Everyone wishes he or she could do a job more easily or have more fun. Inventors try to make those wishes come true. Inventing or improving an invention requires time and patience.

A company in Canada had a better idea in 1895. It invented the first power tool. Today, many other tools are powered by electricity—including this cordless power screwdriver. Today, inventors are still improving power tool technology, including using lasers and microwaves to drill into steel, stone, and glass. Maybe, someday, you will have a better idea for a new power tool.

Cordless Screwdriver
A power screwdriver turns screws with ease. Because it runs on batteries, you can use it anywhere.

Exchangeable Tip

Motor

Batteries

How to Be an Inventor

1 **Identify a problem.** It may be a problem at school, at home, or in your community.

2 **List ways to solve the problem.** Sometimes the solution is a new tool. Other times it may be a new way of doing an old job or activity.

3 **Choose the best solution.** Decide which idea you predict will work best. Think about which one you can carry out.

4 **Make a sample.** A sample, called a *prototype*, is the first try. Your idea may need many materials or none at all. Choose measuring tools that will help your design work better.

5 **Try out your invention.** Use your prototype, or ask some else to try it. Keep a record of how it works and what problems you find. The more times you try it, the more information you will have.

6 **Improve your invention.** Use what you learned to make your design work better. Draw or write about the changes you made and why you made them.

7 **Share your invention.** Show your invention to others. Explain how it works. Tell how it makes an activity easier or more fun. If it did not work as well as you wanted, tell why.

Make Decisions

Trouble for Manatees

Manatees are large, slow-moving marine mammals. An average manatee is about 3 meters long and has a mass of about 500 kilograms. Manatees are gentle plant eaters.

In summer, manatees can be seen along the ocean coasts of Alabama, Georgia, Florida, and South Carolina. In winter, they migrate to the warm waters of bays and rivers along the Gulf Coast of Florida. Living near the coast protects the manatees from diseases they might catch in colder waters. However, there are dangers in living so close to land. The great majority of manatee deaths are caused by collisions with boats. Almost all manatees have scars on their backs from being hit by fast-moving boats.

Deciding What to Do

What can be done to protect manatees from harm?

Here's how to make your decision about the manatees. You can use the same steps to help solve problems in your home, in your school, and in your community.

1 **LEARN** Learn about the problem. Take the time needed to get the facts. You could talk to an expert, read a science book, or explore a website.

2 **LIST** Make a list of actions you could take. Add actions other people could take.

3 **DECIDE** Think about each action on your list. Identify the risks and benefits. Decide which choice is the best one for you, your school or your community.

4 **SHARE** Communicate your decision to others.

Boat Slow Speed Zone!

Science Safety

☑ Know the safety rules of your school and classroom and follow them.

☑ Read and follow the safety tips in each Investigate activity.

☑ When you plan your own investigations, write down how to keep safe.

☑ Know how to clean up and put away science materials. Keep your work area clean, and tell your teacher about spills right away.

☑ Know how to safely plug in electrical devices.

☑ Wear safety goggles when your teacher tells you.

☑ Unless your teacher tells you to, never put any science materials in or near your ears, eyes, or mouth.

☑ Wear gloves when handling live animals.

☑ Wash your hands when your investigation is done.

Caring for Living Things

☑ Learn how to care for the plants and animals in your classroom so that they stay healthy and safe. Learn how to hold animals carefully.

LIFE UNIT **B** SCIENCE

Interactions
Among
Living Things

Interactions Among Living Things

Independent Reading

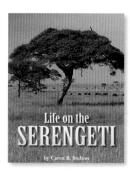

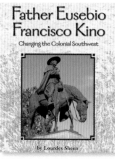

**Life on the
Serengeti**

Biomes

**Father Eusebio
Francisco Kino**

Discover!

The ears of a jackrabbit measure one-third the length of its body! How do long ears help a jackrabbit survive in hot places? In this unit, you'll learn how certain characteristics help animals survive in their native habitats.

Chapter 4

Ecosystems, Communities, and Biomes

LESSON

1

Sunlight, water, air, plants, animals, and you—how do you and other living things interact with the environment?

Read about it in Lesson 1.

LESSON

2

Lots of rain or plenty of sunshine—in which type of biome do you live?

Read about it in Lesson 2.

LESSON

3

Producers, consumers, decomposers—can you find your way around a food web?

Read about it in Lesson 3.

How Do Living Things Form Communities?

Why It Matters...

You live in a community made up of trees and grasses, pets and people, and all the other living things in your area. Living things interact with one another and with nonliving things. In nature, everything an animal needs to survive—including food, air, and shelter—comes from the living and nonliving things in its environment.

PREPARE TO INVESTIGATE

Inquiry Skill

Observe When you observe, you use your senses to determine and describe the properties of objects and events.

Materials

- soil
- 500 ml beaker
- terrarium
- organic matter, such as peat moss or decayed leaves
- food scraps
- water
- earthworms

Look at Life

Procedure

Safety: Wash your hands after setting up the terrarium.

STEP 1

1. **Collaborate** Work in a small group. Measure 500 ml of soil in the beaker. Pour the soil into the terrarium. Spread a thin layer of organic matter over the soil. Add earthworms and a handful of food scraps, such as apple peels, to the terrarium.

2. **Predict** Add water to one side of the terrarium until the soil is slightly wet. In your *Science Notebook,* predict how the earthworms will react to the water. Loosely place the lid on the terrarium. Place it out of the sunlight.

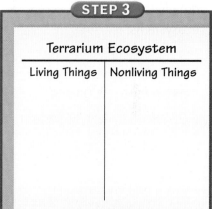
STEP 3

Terrarium Ecosystem	
Living Things	Nonliving Things

3. **Classify** Make a chart in your *Science Notebook* like the one shown. Classify the things in the terrarium as living or nonliving.

4. **Observe** Each day for one week, carefully observe the earthworms and their environment.

STEP 4

5. **Record Data** Write down your observations in your *Science Notebook.* Include the time and day of each observation.

Conclusion

1. **Observe** What interactions did you observe between the earthworms and their environment?

2. **Infer** Based on your observations, what do earthworms need to survive?

Investigate More!

Design an Experiment
Predict whether earthworms grow largest in fine, coarse, or rocky soil. How could you test your prediction? Run an experiment with your teacher's approval.

Ecosystems

MAIN IDEA An ecosystem is a community of different plants and animals, as well as the water, soil, and other nonliving things in the area.

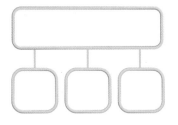
What Is an Ecosystem?

If you put your head on the ground of a forest, what would you see? You might notice ants marching in line, or worms burrowing through the soil. Fuzzy mosses might tickle your nose, and twigs and bits of leaves might stick in your hair.

A section of forest floor is one example of an ecosystem. An **ecosystem** is made up of all the living and nonliving things that interact in one place. In a forest, the living things range from tiny bacteria and earthworms to trees towering above. Nonliving things include sunlight, soil, water, and air.

Scientists define and study small ecosystems, such as a rotting log or a patch of soil under a tree. They also study large ecosystems, such as a large forest or prairie. Regardless of size, everything in an ecosystem interacts.

Small Ecosystems
Soil, a rotting log, fungus, moss, and a lizard are all part of this small ecosystem.

The Florida Everglades is a large ecosystem in southern Florida. The land is swampy, covered by a thin layer of muddy water. Grasses grow tall because only a few cypress trees block the sunlight.

Closer to the ocean, salt water mixes with fresh water in shallow lands called estuaries. Mangrove trees thrive in estuaries, as do newly hatched fish and shrimp. Many birds nest in the mangroves and fish the waters for food.

The plants, birds, fish, and other organisms of the Everglades make up a community. A **community** is the group of living things found in an ecosystem. These living things depend upon one another for food, shelter, and other needs. They also depend upon the nonliving things in the ecosystem.

Organisms that live well in one ecosystem might not survive in another. Alligators, for example, find food and shelter only in warm, wet places. They also must drink lots of water to flush wastes from their blood.

Like the alligator, the roseate spoonbill is well suited for life in the Everglades. Its tall legs and strong feet are ideal for wading. It shakes its open bill through the water to capture small fish and other animals.

▶ **MAIN IDEA** Describe some interactions among living things in the Everglades.

Roseate spoonbill

Florida panther

Alligator

Large Ecosystem
The Florida Everglades includes a community of many living things, including cypress, birds, panthers, and alligators.

Populations

You can learn a great deal by studying an individual plant, animal, or other organism. But to understand how an ecosystem functions, you need to study populations. A **population** consists of all the members of the same type of organism that live in an ecosystem.

The Everglades ecosystem includes populations of mangrove and cypress trees, alligators and spoonbills, and a wide variety of other species. The birth or death of one plant or animal is not likely to change the Everglades very much. But what if a disease killed all the mangrove trees? Or a new animal species began nesting where the spoonbills nest? Events like these can affect the entire community.

To evaluate ecosystems, scientists consider factors that affect the whole community. One major concern for the Everglades is the water supply. The Everglades depends on fresh water flowing from the north. Yet human needs are draining that supply, and those needs are growing every year.

In an ocean ecosystem, which fish would you suspect are most important in the community? Arguably, the answer is the smallest fishes, including herring and mackerel. These fish are food for bigger fish, which in turn are food for sharks, killer whales, and other big animals. Without large numbers of small fish, many other animals would starve.

▶ **MAIN IDEA** Why are small fish important in ocean ecosystems?

Populations in the Ocean

Feeding Relationships
Small fish eat algae and other plant life, and they are food for larger fish. Feeding relationships like these are a part of all ecosystems.

Visual Summary

Ecosystems are made up of all the living and nonliving things that interact in a given place.

A community is made up of different populations of living things in an ecosystem.

A population consists of all the members of the same type of organism that live in a community.

LINKS for Home and School

MATH **Make an Estimate** A stable population of small beach crabs is the primary food source for a certain type of sea bird. The crabs support a population of about 500 birds. Changes in the environment result in a 30 percent increase in the crab population. About how many individuals might one expect to find in the sea bird population in later years?

TECHNOLOGY **Make a Poster** Use the Internet or library to explore which types of technology scientists use to study ecosystems. Share your results with the class by making a poster. Use words and images to explain how the technology works and how it is used.

Review

❶ MAIN IDEA How do scientists classify the parts of an ecosystem?

❷ VOCABULARY Use the terms *ecosystem, community,* and *population* to describe the area where you live.

❸ READING SKILL: Main Idea and Details What nonliving things are found in ecosystems? Why are they important?

❹ CRITICAL THINKING: Apply What might happen if one population in an ecosystem disappeared? Give an example.

❺ INQUIRY SKILL: Observe Go outside with a partner and carefully observe a small patch of grass. Classify the things you observe as living or nonliving.

 TEST PREP

What makes up an ecosystem?

A. plants and animals only

B. water, air, and other nonliving things

C. all the living and nonliving things and their interactions

D. one population only

 Technology
Visit **www.eduplace.com/scp/** to find out more about ecosystems.

What Are Biomes?

Why It Matters...

Is your area usually hot and wet, or cold and dry? Are there thick forests or tall grasses? These types of factors affect many parts of your life, including the kind of home you live in and the clothes that you wear.

All plants and animals are affected by their environments. The prairie dogs shown below live very well on the grasslands, but would not survive on the tundra or in a rainforest. Earth's different regions support different kinds of living things.

PREPARE TO INVESTIGATE

Inquiry Skill

Analyze Data When you analyze data, you look for patterns in the information to make inferences, predictions, and other generalizations.

Materials
- different-colored pencils
- calculator

Science and Math Toolbox
For step 1, review **Making a Line Graph** on page H13.

Compare Climates

Procedure

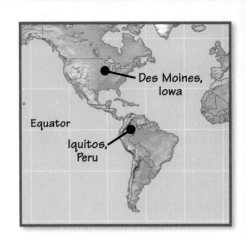

Des Moines, Iowa

Equator

Iquitos, Peru

1 **Use Numbers** In your *Science Notebook* make a line graph using data in the temperature chart for Des Moines, Iowa and Iquitos, Peru. Plot the months on the x-axis and temperature on the y-axis.

2 **Use Numbers** Use the data in the precipitation chart to make a bar graph in your *Science Notebook.* Plot the months on the x-axis and precipitation on the y-axis.

3 **Use Numbers** Calculate average annual rates of precipitation and temperature for both places.

Average Temperature												
	Jan.	Feb.	Mar.	Apr.	May	Jun.	Jul.	Aug.	Sep.	Oct.	Nov.	Dec.
Des Moines	−7°C	−5°C	−3°C	3°C	7°C	21°C	23°C	22°C	18°C	11°C	2°C	−4°C
Iquitos	27°C	26°C	25°C	25°C	25°C	24°C	24°C	25°C	25°C	25°C	26°C	26°C

Average Precipitation												
	Jan.	Feb.	Mar.	Apr.	May	Jun.	Jul.	Aug.	Sep.	Oct.	Nov.	Dec.
Des Moines	4 cm	3 cm	5 cm	6 cm	11 cm	13 cm	8 cm	9 cm	7 cm	6 cm	4 cm	2 cm
Iquitos	24 cm	26 cm	25 cm	35 cm	26 cm	13 cm	16 cm	12 cm	27 cm	19 cm	24 cm	26 cm

Conclusion

1. **Analyze Data** Describe temperature and precipitation patterns in both places. Which place receives more precipitation? Is precipitation constant throughout the year?

2. **Compare** Use the data to compare Des Moines and Iquitos to your community.

Investigate More!

Design an Experiment
Study a globe to find a city of the same latitude as Des Moines. Research climate data for that city. How do their climates compare? Make a chart or graph to show data.

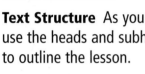

Biomes

MAIN IDEA Biomes are large regions of Earth. Each biome has a characteristic climate that determines its communities of living things.

Earth's Major Biomes

A **biome** is a large group of ecosystems that have similar characteristics. Study the map below to find the six major land biomes.

What makes biomes different from one another? The most important factor is climate. **Climate** refers to the type of weather that occurs in an area over a long period of time. Some climates are rainy, while others are quite dry. Some have a variety of temperatures, while others are almost always hot or cold. Different climates support different populations of living things.

Earth is home to six major land biomes. In each biome, climate affects the kinds of plants and animals that live there. ▼

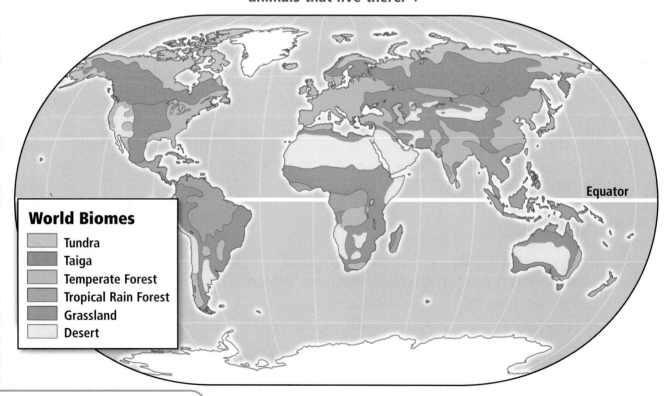

World Biomes
- Tundra
- Taiga
- Temperate Forest
- Tropical Rain Forest
- Grassland
- Desert

Equator

Forest Biomes

Forests are home to tall trees and the animals that live in them. Forests are part of two biomes. **Tropical rain forests** are very rainy and hot. Some rain forests get more than 600 cm (240 in.) of rain each year! Temperatures range from about 18°C to 35°C (64°F to 95°F), which is like a hot summer that lasts all year.

Because of the moisture and warmth, tropical rain forests are teeming with life. In fact, more kinds of plants and animals live in this biome than in any other. Its huge mass of plants produces much of Earth's oxygen. Some of these plants might supply new medicines and other useful products.

The other type of forest biome, **temperate forests,** experiences four distinct seasons: summer, fall, winter, and spring. Temperatures range from a chilly –30°C (–22°F) to a warm 30°C (86°F). A temperate forest receives perhaps one-fifth the rainfall of a tropical forest.

These forests are home to animals such as white-tailed deer, rabbits, skunks, squirrels, and black bears. The trees include maple, oak, hickory, and beech. These trees lose their leaves in the fall and are dormant through winter. The fallen leaves decay on the ground and add nutrients to the soil.

▶ **TEXT STRUCTURE** Compare the climates of both forests.

Tropical Rain Forest

Location: near the equator
Climate: warm and wet

Temperate Forest

Location: eastern North America and other places
Climate: four distinct seasons

Grasslands

Location: central Africa, central U.S., and other regions

Climate: distinct dry season

Desert

Location: varies

Climate: extremely dry

Grasslands and Deserts

Grasses cover the land in the **grasslands** biome. Trees are few and far between.

There are two main types of grasslands: prairies and savannas. Prairies are found in temperate regions, such as the central United States. Temperatures may dip as low as −40°C (−40°F) in winter and soar to 38°C (100°F) in summer. Prairie animals include prairie dogs, coyotes, hawks, and grouse.

Most savannas are found in warmer regions, such as central Africa. Yearly temperatures typically remain above 18°C (64°F). Elephants, giraffes, lions, and zebras call the savanna home.

A savanna receives as much as 100 cm (40 in.) of rain each year. But the savanna has a dry season, as do other grasslands. That's partly why trees are scarce in this biome—they do not thrive for long periods without water.

The **desert** is the driest biome. Most deserts receive less than 25 cm (10 in.) of rain each year. In fact, some deserts may not see a drop of rain all year long.

Cacti, sagebrush, and other plants are found in many deserts. Desert plants and animals are adapted to live with little water. Cacti, for example, have a waxy coating and spiny leaves to help reduce water loss. Earth's driest deserts contain little life. These deserts are filled with sandy dunes that stretch seemingly without end.

Taiga and Tundra

The **taiga** biome has long, severe winters and short, cool summers. Temperatures may reach 10°C (50°F) during only one to three months each year. The taiga is fairly dry, each year receiving only about 50 cm (20 in.) of precipitation, mostly snow.

The most common trees in the taiga are conifers, such as pines, firs, and spruces. The leaves of these trees are thin, waxy needles that help keep in water. Their leaves do not fall all at once when the weather turns cold. Animals of the taiga include moose, deer, and wolves.

As harsh as the taiga can be, it is mild compared to the tundra. The **tundra** is Earth's coldest biome, having an average winter temperature of –34°C (–29°F). The ground is frozen for hundreds of meters down, and lower layers stay frozen all year long. This frozen ground is called permafrost.

In summer, temperatures hover just under 10°C (50°F). As the ground thaws, the tundra becomes swampy and covered with mosses, lichens, and dwarf-like trees. Mosquitoes thrive in the short summer.

Other tundra animals include polar bears, caribou, and reindeer. These animals have adaptations that help them survive in this cold biome. Polar bears, for example, have a thick layer of fat to keep them warm.

▶ **TEXT STRUCTURE** How do temperatures compare in the taiga and tundra?

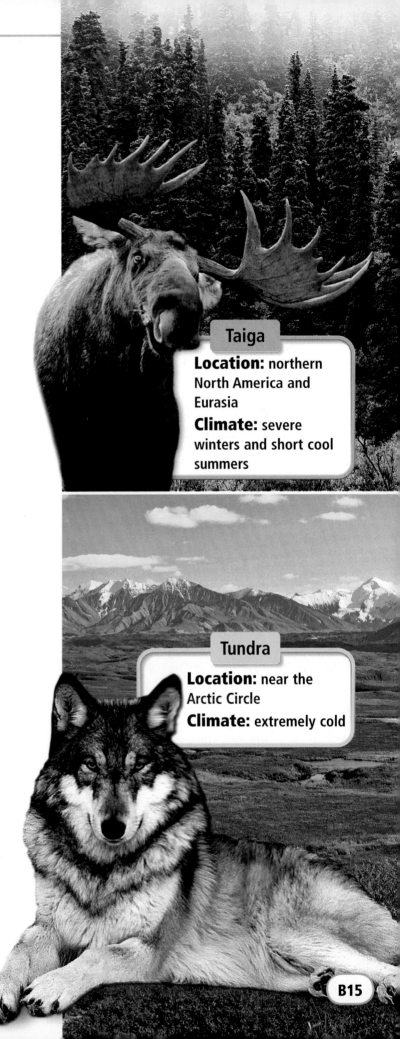

Taiga
Location: northern North America and Eurasia
Climate: severe winters and short cool summers

Tundra
Location: near the Arctic Circle
Climate: extremely cold

Marine Biomes

Look back at the map on page B12. Oceans cover about 70 percent of Earth's surface! They are home to the marine biomes.

Living things need special adaptations to live on or near the ocean shore. This is because the water level keeps changing with the tides. The intertidal zone is the area that ocean tides cover and uncover in a regular cycle. Sometimes this zone is under water, and other times it is exposed to the Sun and air.

In this zone, animals such as clams and mussels attach sticky threads to rocks so the waves won't wash them away. Other animals, including many kinds of crabs and some snails, can move about over land and underwater.

Just beyond the shore is the near-shore zone. In some places, this zone is home to an underground forest of tall, brown seaweed called kelp. Otters and other animals live among the swaying stalks.

The presence of water and sunlight defines the zones of marine biomes. Different plants and animals live in each. ▼

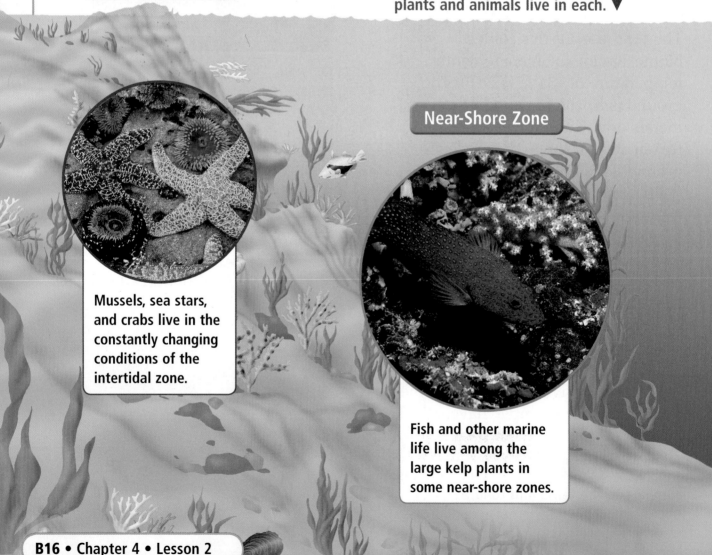

Intertidal Zone

Mussels, sea stars, and crabs live in the constantly changing conditions of the intertidal zone.

Near-Shore Zone

Fish and other marine life live among the large kelp plants in some near-shore zones.

Still farther out to sea is the open ocean zone. Here, the water is deep and cold. Tiny algae float near the surface. Algae are plant-like organisms, and most are single-celled. Because algae are so numerous, they produce most of Earth's oxygen! They also provide food for ocean animals.

Even when the water is clear, sunlight mostly reaches a depth of only about 200 meters (660 ft). So, the floor of the open ocean is very cold and dark. Organisms here use special adaptations to survive such a harsh environment. Some fish produce their own light, just as lightning bugs do on land. The light helps them to hunt for food.

Other unusual organisms include the giant tubeworms that live by vents on the ocean floor. These vents release heat and gases from Earth's interior. The tubeworms are unusual because the vents—not the Sun—are the source of their energy. Bacteria near the vents make food using heated chemicals, a process unlike any other on Earth.

▶ **TEXT STRUCTURE** **Compare the conditions in the three zones of the ocean.**

Dolphins, whales, and jellyfish spend much of their time near the surface in open ocean zones.

Open Ocean Zone

Huge schools of herring, tuna, and other fish live in the middle depths of the open ocean.

Fangtooth fish and other creatures have adapted to the cold and darkness of the deepest parts of the ocean.

Freshwater Ecosystems

Other bodies of water are made up of fresh water. These ecosystems include streams, rivers, ponds, lakes, and wetlands.

Streams and rivers contain flowing water. Near the beginning of a river, the current is usually fast and the water is clear. Trout and other fast-swimming fish live in this zone. Farther downstream, the current slows and the river widens. Plants are able to take root in the muddy bottom. Fish, beavers, and waterfowl may find homes here.

Kingfishers hunt for fish in fresh water. ▼

As the river flows, it picks up sediments. Near the end of the river, called the mouth, the water drops its sediments and becomes murky. Catfish and carp may live in these dark waters.

Ponds and lakes are made of still water. Some are small and may disappear during dry spells. Others, such as the Great Lakes, are huge.

Deep ponds and lakes have three different zones. Algae, plants, insects, and fish live near the sun-warmed surface. Farther down, the water is cooler, but some sunlight shines through. Here live plankton, which is a general term for many kinds of tiny organisms that live in water. Fish and other larger animals feed on the plankton.

Still farther down is a zone that is deep and cold. Bacteria and other decomposers break down dead plants and animals.

▶ **TEXT STRUCTURE** What are three types of freshwater ecosystems?

Visual Summary

Different biomes have different climates and types of plants. Climate is influenced by temperature and precipitation.

Land biomes include tropical rain forests, temperate forests, grasslands, deserts, taiga, and tundra.

Water covers much of Earth's surface. Many organisms live in marine biomes and freshwater ecosystems.

LINKS for Home and School

MATH **Find an Average** Annual rainfall in a particular rain forest is shown in the table below. What was the average rainfall over the five-year period?

Year 1	Year 2	Year 3	Year 4	Year 5
250 cm	240 cm	230 cm	260 cm	250 cm

TECHNOLOGY **Gather Data** Set up a rain gauge and record precipitation levels for one week. During the same period, use a thermometer to record temperatures. Explain how your data relate to the type of climate found in your biome.

Review

① **MAIN IDEA** What factors distinguish one biome from another?

② **VOCABULARY** What is a biome? List six examples of biomes.

③ **READING SKILL: Text Structure** Use your outline of this lesson to summarize the biome of your choice.

④ **CRITICAL THINKING: Analyze** Why aren't marine algae found at depths below 200 meters? How does this influence life at these depths?

⑤ **INQUIRY SKILL: Analyze Data** Which land biomes have a greater temperature range during the year, those near the equator or those in temperate regions?

 TEST PREP

Unlike freshwater ecosystems, marine biomes are

A. salty.

B. dry.

C. sunny.

D. full of life.

 Technology

Visit **www.eduplace.com/scp/** to find out more about biomes.

Earth's ecosystems inspire writers of both fiction and science. Compare these two selections about the Everglades of Florida.

Some Rivers

by Frank Asch

Some rivers rush to the sea.
They push and tumble and fall.
But the Everglades is a river
with no hurry in her at all.
Soaking the cypress
that grows so tall;
nursing a frog,
so quiet and small;
she flows but a mile
in the course of a day,
with plenty of time
to think on the way.

But how can she cope
with the acres of corn
and sorrowful cities that drain her?
With hunters and tourists and levees
that chain and stain and pain her?
Does the half of her that's left
think only of the past?
Or does she think of her future
and how long it will last?
Some rivers rush to the sea.
They push and tumble and fall.
But the Everglades is a river
with no hurry in her at all.

The River of Grass

Prologue to Everglades: Buffalo Tiger and the River of Grass, **by Peter Lourie**

In the early sixteenth century the Spanish explorer Ponce de León searched the coast of Florida for the Fountain of Youth. He never discovered the mythical fountain, but if he had penetrated deeper into the peninsula that the Spaniards called "the land of flowers," he might have found something else: the Everglades, a slow-moving swamp that is in fact a huge, silent river.

The Everglades, called Pa-hay-okee, or "Grassy Water," by the Miccosukee Indians, is often only inches deep, yet it runs a hundred miles from Florida's Lake Okeechobee to the Gulf of Mexico and Florida Bay. In places it is seventy miles wide. It has been called a river of grass because of the dense waves of tawny sawgrass arcing gently to the south, pointing in the direction of the sluggish flow of the water.

The Miccosukee Indians have lived in the Everglades for more than a hundred years. When they first arrived they found the river of grass to be a kind of paradise. Even today, the Grassy Water dazzles the eye with its abundance of birds and other wildlife. Yet, unlike a hundred years ago, there is sadness in this bright spot on the planet. Great pressures from pollution and overdevelopment threaten to destroy the river of grass.

Sharing Ideas

1. **READING CHECK** According to both passages, what major problems threaten the Everglades?

2. **WRITE ABOUT IT** Why is the Everglades a special, unique place? Express your ideas.

3. **TALK ABOUT IT** What

What Is a Food Web?

Why It Matters...

What did you have for breakfast? Like this owl, you get the energy you need from food. Food energy comes ultimately from the Sun. It is then passed through an ecosystem by living things.

Inquiry Skill

Use Models When you use models, you make and analyze a structure or picture representing a real-world process to better understand how the process works.

Materials

- different-colored pencils
- Investigate photo card

Science and Math Toolbox
For step 2, review **Making a Chart to Organize Data** on page H11.

Model Energy Flow

Procedure

1 **Hypothesize** Look at the photo card of living things. It includes grass, zebras, and a lion. Form a hypothesis about how each organism obtains its energy.

2 **Use Models** In an ecosystem, energy from food passes from one organism to another. Producers get their energy from the Sun. In your *Science Notebook,* make a chart like the one shown. Which organisms in the photo are producers? Draw the producers in the bottom level of the chart.

3 **Use Numbers** Producers get 100 units of energy from the Sun. Write this number of units on the chart. Note that producers use 90 percent of these units for their own life processes.

4 **Use Models** Which consumers eat the producers? Draw the consumers in the next level of the chart. Record the amount of energy available to them. They will use 90 percent of this energy.

5 **Use Models** Which consumer eats other consumers? Draw this consumer in the top level of the chart. Record its available energy.

Conclusion

1. **Use Numbers** How much energy is left for the living things that eat the producers? How much is left for the last consumer?

2. **Infer** Why aren't there more levels in the chart? Explain.

STEP 1

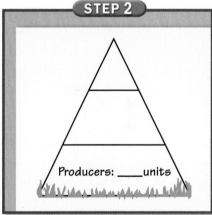

STEP 2

Producers: _____units

Investigate More!

Research The model you used is called an energy pyramid. Use the Internet or library to research energy pyramids. What happens to energy as it is passed from one living thing to another?

VOCABULARY

food chain   p. B25
food web   p. B26

READING SKILL

Classify As you read, sort groups of living things according to their role in a food web.

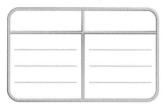

Energy Flow

MAIN IDEA In an ecosystem, energy flows from producers to consumers to decomposers.

Energy from Food

Would you like to make food from a gas in the air and water from the ground? You could do that—if you were a plant. Plants are Earth's producers, as are algae and certain bacteria. A producer makes its own food from raw materials and energy.

Plants and other producers use the energy of sunlight, changing it into chemical energy. Water and carbon dioxide combine into sugars and oxygen. Sugars are the food for the plant. Plants use some of these sugars to grow, and store the rest in their tissues.

When you eat a plant, you take in energy the plant stored. You and all other animals are consumers. A consumer gets energy by eating food, not producing it.

First-Level Consumer

The caterpillar is a first-level consumer that eats leaves.

Producer

Grass and other plants are producers. They make up the first link in most food chains.

Food Chains

To better understand feeding relationships, scientists organize the living things of a community into food chains. A **food chain** describes how energy in an ecosystem flows from one organism to another.

Almost all food chains begin with the Sun. Producers, such as green grass, capture the Sun's energy to make food. Animals that eat plants, such as a caterpillar, are called first-level consumers or primary consumers. These animals eat plants or other producers.

The birds are second-level consumers. They eat other consumers. The cat is a third-level consumer. Notice that all the consumers rely on plants. Without plants, there would not be a food chain.

Which other organisms play a role in a food chain? If plants and animals die without being eaten, organisms called decomposers will break down the remains. Decomposers include bacteria, some protists, and fungi, as well as earthworms and other small animals. They serve to return an organism's tissues back to the soil for new organisms to use again.

In every ecosystem, different producers, consumers, and decomposers are constantly filling their roles in food chains. You, too, are part of food chains. When are you a primary consumer? Are you also a second-level consumer?

> **CLASSIFY** Compare a producer and a consumer.

Second-Level Consumer

The bird is a second-level consumer that eats the caterpillar.

Third-Level Consumer

The cat is a third-level consumer that eats the bird.

Decomposers

Decomposers break down the decaying remains of dead producers and consumers.

Food Webs

Like you, most animals take part in more than one food chain. For example, do cats eat only birds? No, cats also eat mice and fish.

A **food web** shows how food chains combine in an ecosystem. Look at the food web on the opposite page. The algae, trees, and smaller plants are producers. The mouse eats plant seeds, and it also eats insects. The snake eats insects, too, but it also eats mice. The hawk hunts both mice and snakes, and so does the fox.

By studying food webs, scientists can explain how ecosystems function. They also can predict the effects of changes to an ecosystem. If the hawks all left the ecosystem shown here, how do you think the other animals would be affected?

Classifying Consumers Most consumers play a similar role in every food chain they are a part of. A rabbit, for example, is always a primary consumer. It is an herbivore, meaning "plant eater."

Other consumers are second- or third-level consumers. Examples include hawks and snakes. These animals are called carnivores. The word *carnivore* means "meat eater." Many carnivores are predators, animals that hunt and kill prey.

A few animals, such as bears, eat both plants and animals. They are omnivores—the prefix *omni-* meaning "all." If you eat both plant and animal products, you are an omnivore, too.

Cycles in Nature

Food chains and food webs show how energy flows through an ecosystem. Ecosystems have many other interactions, too.

For example, as you learned in Chapter 2, plants take up carbon dioxide from the air and release oxygen. Animals do just the opposite—they release carbon dioxide and take in oxygen. In this way, plants and animals provide one another with the gases each needs.

Another important cycle is the water cycle. All living things need water. Water leaves Earth's surface through evaporation. It returns through rain, sleet, and snow.

Nitrogen also cycles through ecosystems. Nitrogen is a gas that makes up almost four-fifths of Earth's atmosphere. All living things need nitrogen, but in a form different than nitrogen gas from the air. Fortunately, certain bacteria are able to "fix" nitrogen gas into a form that plants can use. Animals obtain nitrogen by eating plants.

Bug-eating Plants Marshy soils typically have little fixed nitrogen. To get the nitrogen they need, some plants take an interesting approach— they "eat" animals!

When an insect touches the tooth-like fringes on a Venus flytrap, for example, the plant closes its leaves over it. These plants trap insects not for their energy, but for the fixed nitrogen in their bodies.

▶ **CLASSIFY** How do consumers and producers interact in an ecosystem?

Food Web

Energy is transferred from one organism to another in a food web. The arrows show the direction of energy flow.

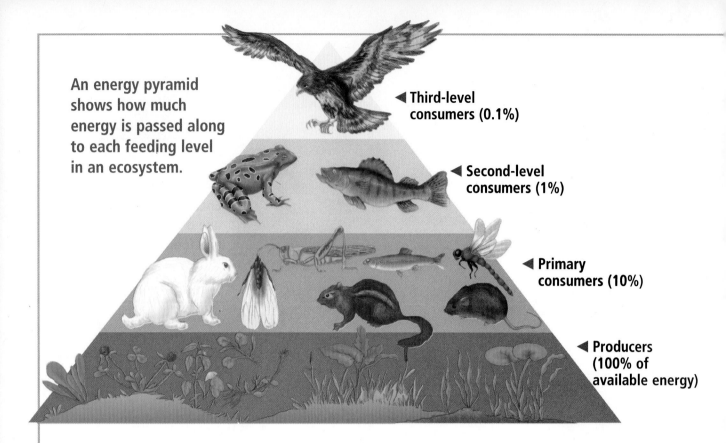

An energy pyramid shows how much energy is passed along to each feeding level in an ecosystem.

◄ Third-level consumers (0.1%)

◄ Second-level consumers (1%)

◄ Primary consumers (10%)

◄ Producers (100% of available energy)

Energy Pyramid

What happens to the food you eat? You use the energy stored in food to walk, run, and engage in many other activities. A lot of this energy leaves your body in the form of heat. Any leftover energy is stored in your body tissues. You, like all living things, use some energy, lose some as heat, and store some energy in tissues.

An energy pyramid shows how energy flows through an ecosystem. Notice that each level is larger than the level above it. In general, only about 10 percent of the energy in one level is passed on to the next.

Producers, such as plants, make up the base of the energy pyramid. Primary consumers make up the next level. Second- and third-level consumers make up the next levels.

An energy pyramid explains a great deal about the populations of ecosystems. As a general rule, producers have the largest populations because they have the most energy available to them. Next in numbers are the primary and second-level consumers. An ecosystem can support only a few third-level consumers.

The higher an animal's level on the energy pyramid, the wider the range of land it must cover for food. This explains the large hunting ranges of animals such as eagles, lions, and snakes. These animals all have adaptations to move quickly and to catch smaller animals.

The energy pyramid also explains why food chains last only for three or four links. Beyond that, little energy remains for an animal to use.

 **CLASSIFY** **What is an energy pyramid?**

Lesson Wrap-Up

Visual Summary

Producers get their energy from the Sun. All other living things get their energy from producers.

A food chain shows the flow of energy from one organism to another. A food web shows overlapping food chains in an ecosystem.

Energy is lost as heat at each step of a food chain. An energy pyramid shows how much energy is available for producers and consumers.

LINKS for Home and School

MATH **Make a Graph** Only 10 percent of the energy in one level of a food chain is passed on to the next. Make a graph showing energy movement in a four-level food chain. Assume 100 units of energy at the lowest level.

HEALTH **Make a Food Pyramid** Humans need to eat different types of foods to stay healthy. Research the basic food groups and serving suggestions. Make a food pyramid that shows what you should eat each day.

Review

1 **MAIN IDEA** Describe how energy flows through an ecosystem.

2 **VOCABULARY** Compare a food chain with a food web. Use both terms to explain how animals interact and depend on one another.

3 **READING SKILL: Classify** Give one example each of a producer, herbivore, carnivore, omnivore, and decomposer.

4 **CRITICAL THINKING: Apply** What would happen to an ecosystem if a drought killed half of the plants that lived there?

5 **INQUIRY SKILL: Use Models** List the things you ate for breakfast today. Use the list to construct one or more food chains for each food.

 TEST PREP
Unlike a carnivore, an herbivore

A. makes its own food.

B. eats only producers.

C. eats other animals.

D. eats both plants and animals.

 Technology
Visit **www.eduplace.com/scp/** to find out more about food webs.

Blushing Giants

Walruses blush a lot, but not because they're embarrassed! It's just their way of staying comfortable in their cold Arctic biome. Walruses have a thick layer of blubber that keeps them warm in the ocean. Out in the Sun, all that padding makes them hot. So when they sunbathe, their hot blood rushes to the surface to let off some heat. The walruses turn bright pink.

Hippopotamuses turn pink too, but in a very different way. Hippo skin oozes reddish slime. This slime is an adaptation to the hot climate of their African biome. The slime keeps the hippos' skin from drying out under the powerful tropical sun. It works as a sunscreen too. The best part is that the hippo never has to remember to put it on!

Keeping cool is a full-time job for hippos. All day they do little but wade. They don't even eat. Only at sundown do they lumber out of the river to graze in comfort on the grasslands.

These overgrown teeth are no use at all for chewing, but they make handy tools in a frozen world. After a huge meal of clams on the ocean floor, walruses use their sharp tusks to haul themselves onto the slippery ice.

Vocabulary

Complete each sentence with a term from the list.

1. A(n) _____ shows overlapping food chains in an ecosystem.

2. Zebras are an example of a(n) _____ of living things in an ecosystem.

3. The flow of energy from producer to first-level consumer to second-level consumer can be shown using a simple _____.

4. Different populations of living things found in the same area at the same time form a(n) _____.

5. A(n) _____ includes living and nonliving things interacting together.

6. Ecosystems with similar climate and vegetation make up a(n) _____.

7. Temperature and precipitation determine the _____ of an area.

8. The _____ biome has long, severe winters and short, cool summers.

9. Prairies and savannas are the two main types of _____.

10. _____ has a layer of frozen ground called permafrost.

biome B12
community B7
climate B12
desert B14
ecosystem B6
food chain B25
food web B26
grasslands B14
population B8
taiga B15
temperate forests B13
tropical rain forests B13
tundra B15

Test Prep

Write the letter of the best answer choice.

11. About _____ percent of the energy available at one level of an energy pyramid passes to the next level.

  A. 10
  B. 30
  C. 60
  D. 90

12. Tropical rain forests are _____ year round.

  A. cold and dry
  B. cold and wet
  C. warm and dry
  D. warm and wet

13. Very limited populations survive in Earth's driest _____.

  A. tropical rain forests
  B. grasslands
  C. taigas
  D. deserts

14. Trees that lose their leaves in cool fall weather are common in _____.

  A. tropical rain forests
  B. temperate rain forests
  C. taigas
  D. deserts

Inquiry Skills

15. Classify How do scientists classify a marine biome into three zones? In which zone must populations survive both above and below the water? What happens in this zone?

16. Analyze Data The table below shows climate data for two cities in the United States. What biome do you suspect each city is a part of? Explain. You may choose to graph the data to organize it.

Temp: Average monthly temperature (°F)
Precip: Total precipitation (inches)

Month	City A Temp/Precip.	City B Temp/Precip.
Jan.	54/0.7	24/2.7
March	62/0.9	34/2.7
May	79/0.1	57/3.1
July	94/0.8	71/3.1
Sept.	86/0.9	62/3.5
Nov.	62/0.7	41/3.8

Critical Thinking

17. Apply Describe four ways that you interacted with living and nonliving things in ecosystems today.

18. Analyze If you wanted to show energy flow in an ecosystem, would it be best to use a food chain or a food web? Explain your answer.

19. Evaluate Your friend comments that bacteria are all unhealthy. What could you say to improve his understanding of bacteria?

20. Analyze Which animal receives more energy from a producer: a first-level consumer or a second-level consumer? Explain.

Performance Assessment

Display a Biome

Make a display that shows a typical scene from a biome. Include at least four different types of living things. The display may be a detailed drawing, poster, or diorama. Write a paragraph or short essay to accompany the display.

Map the Concept

Fill the terms below into the concept map. Each oval represents a larger group than the oval inside it.

Biome
Community
Ecosystem
Organism
Population

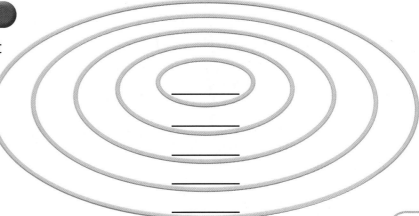

Chapter 5

Life in Ecosystems

Lesson Preview

LESSON

1

Living things live on the highest mountains and in the deepest oceans. How do they survive in such different places?

Read about it in Lesson 1.

LESSON

2

Decreases in food supply, changes in climate, relocated species—how do these factors upset the balance of an ecosystem?

Read about it in Lesson 2.

LESSON

3

Swamps turn into meadows, meadows turn into forests—how do living things respond to changes in ecosystems?

Read about it in Lesson 3.

What Are Habitats and Niches?

Why It Matters...

How can a clownfish live so close to the stinging tentacles of a sea anemone? The fish rubs against the anemone, coating its scales with a kind of slime. The anemone doesn't recognize the coated fish as food.

Living things interact with one another in all sorts of ways. These interactions are key to understanding how they survive.

PREPARE TO INVESTIGATE

Inquiry Skill

Observe When you observe, you use your senses to describe the properties of objects and events.

Materials

- safety goggles
- earthworms
- goldfish
- 2 aquariums
- soil
- organic matter
- apple peels
- fish food

Worm and Fish Habitats

Procedure

Safety: Wear goggles when handling soil.

1. **Collaborate** Work in a small group. Half fill one aquarium with soil. Spread a thin layer of decayed leaves or other organic matter over the soil. Add some earthworms and a handful of apple peels. Moisten the soil. Wash your hands afterwards.

2. **Measure** Fill the second aquarium with water at room temperature, almost to the top. Add the goldfish and fish food. You may also add small rocks and plastic plants. Wash your hands afterwards.

3. **Observe** Each day for a week, observe the earthworms and fish. How do they move? What do they eat? How do they affect their environment?

4. **Record Data** In your *Science Notebook,* write your observations in a chart like the one shown.

Conclusion

1. **Infer** What body parts make the fish well suited to their environment? How are the earthworms suited to their environment?

2. **Predict** Could the fish live in the earthworms' environment? Could the earthworms live in the fish's environment? Why or why not?

STEP 1

STEP 2

STEP 4

Observations		
	Worms	Fish
Physical Properties		
Type of Food		
Interactions		

Investigate More!

Research Learn about an interesting plant or animal that lives in the wild in your state. Where does it live? What role does it fill in its ecosystem?

VOCABULARY

adaptation	p. B40
habitat	p. B38
niche	p. B39
symbiosis	p. B42

READING SKILL

Compare and Contrast
As you read, compare and contrast relationships among different organisms and their environments.

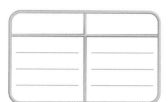

Habitats and Niches

MAIN IDEA Each kind of organism occupies a particular niche in its habitat.

Habitats

To tell people where you live, you probably use a street address. An address is a simple way to describe the location of your home.

All living things have an "address," a place they live in. This place is called a habitat. A **habitat** is the area where an organism lives, grows, and develops. Everything that an organism needs to survive can be found in its habitat.

Many different living things may live in the same habitat. The African savanna, for example, is home to zebras, lions, and many other animals.

Savanna Habitat

Lion
The niche of a lion in a savanna includes hunting zebras.

Niches

Have you seen pictures or movies of workers at an automobile factory? Every worker has a place to be and a job to do. If one of them fails to do his or her job, everyone else's job is affected.

Organisms in a habitat have specific functions, too. A **niche** describes what an organism does in its habitat. You can think of a niche as a job at a factory or a role in a play. Each organism plays a certain role in its habitat.

Look at the savanna habitat shown below. The zebras are consumers. They eat producers, such as grass. They drink water from the watering hole. These are parts of their niche.

Zebras are also food for lions. That is another part of their niche. Zebras and lions share the same habitat, but have different niches.

Niches describe more than just feeding relationships. A niche includes exactly where in the habitat an organism lives, how it reproduces, how it protects itself, and how it behaves. For example, birds in the savanna may live in nests. They may use sticks, mud, and other materials. Part of their niche includes recycling such materials from their habitat.

Each group of organisms in a habitat uses resources in different ways. Zebras, for example, eat the grass. Lions do not eat grass, but they lie in the grass. Birds use the grass to build nests. Because each group uses the same resources in different ways, there are enough resources for everyone. However, changes in ecosystems can upset this balance, as you'll learn in the next lesson.

▶ **COMPARE AND CONTRAST** How do habitats and niches compare?

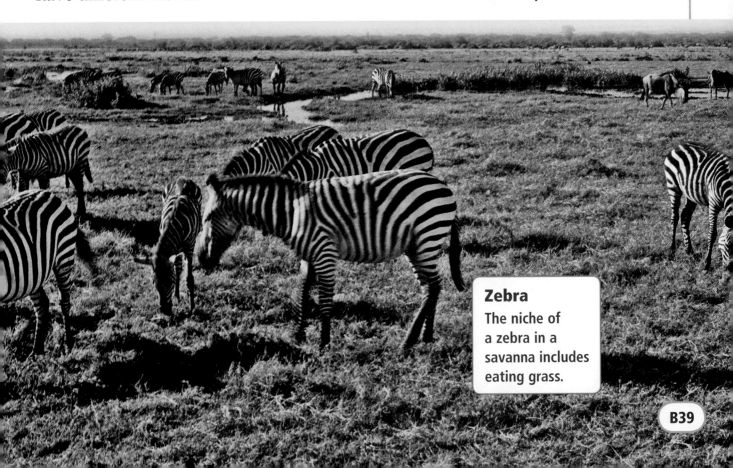

Zebra
The niche of a zebra in a savanna includes eating grass.

Adaptations

What if you see a drawing of a large, white polar bear crossing a hot, sandy desert? Something's wrong with this picture! Can you explain what it is?

The thick fur and heavy padding of a polar bear help it stay warm in its cold, arctic habitat. Desert animals, on the other hand, have body parts that help them stay cool. These characteristics are called adaptations. An **adaptation** is any characteristic that helps an organism survive.

Sometimes adaptations are physical. The turtles in the pictures on this page are good examples of similar animals with different adaptations. The desert tortoise has legs that help it move easily across the sand. The sea turtle has flippers that help it move through water. Each animal's body is physically adapted to its habitat.

Plants have adaptations, too. For example, a cactus's leaves are thin, pointed spines. Its body, or stem, has a very thick outer layer. These adaptations help the cactus conserve water in its dry habitat.

Other adaptations are behavioral. This means that the organism has certain behaviors that help it survive in its habitat. A bat, for example, might sleep through the winter. This adaptation, called hibernation, allows the bat to live in cold climates.

Sea Turtle ▲
The flippers of a sea turtle are adapted for swimming.

Desert Tortoise ▲
The feet of a desert tortoise are adapted for walking in sand.

Cacti
Most plants would wilt and die in a hot desert. Cacti survive because of their waxy stems, long roots, and other adaptations. ▶

Natural Selection

How do organisms develop adaptations? In the mid-1800s, British naturalist Charles Darwin proposed a theory to help explain the process. According to Darwin, some members of a species have characteristics better suited to the environment than other members. These individuals are more likely to survive and pass on their characteristics to their offspring.

This process is known as natural selection. Let's examine how it works.

Picture a rocky beach. A population of birds searches among the rocks for food. Some of the birds have long, pointed beaks and can easily pick up pieces of food from cracks between the rocks. Other birds have shorter, more rounded beaks and cannot reach food.

Which birds are more likely to survive on the rocky beach? Which birds are more likely to reproduce? The birds with the pointed beaks are more likely to do both. Thus, their characteristics are passed on to their offspring. After several generations, many more of the birds on the beach will have pointed beaks.

Most scientists believe that natural selection accounts for the amazing variety of living things and their adaptations. Scientists also use the theory to predict how species might change in the future.

▲ Why does a sandpiper have such a long, thin beak? According to the theory of natural selection, traits that help an animal survive become more common in the population.

The dense, shaggy hair of these yaks helps them survive the bitterly cold weather of the Himalaya Mountains. ▼

▶ **COMPARE AND CONTRAST** What is an adaptation? Compare adaptations among different organisms.

Types of Symbiosis

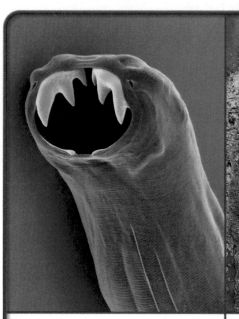

Parasitism
A hookworm takes blood and nutrients from its host. It benefits, and the host is harmed.

Commensalism
An elf owl makes its nest in a hole in a cactus. The owl benefits, and the cactus is not affected.

Mutualism
Cleaner shrimp eat parasites attached to fish. Both the shrimp and the fish benefit from this relationship.

Symbiosis

All living things depend on and affect one another. Sometimes the relationship is very close. **Symbiosis** describes a close, long-lasting relationship between two different kinds of organisms. This word means "living together."

Parasitism is one type of symbiosis. One organism, called the parasite, benefits from living off the body of another organism, the host. For example, a hookworm benefits from living inside the digestive tract of a larger host, such as a dog. The dog may become ill, but it usually doesn't die. If it did, the hookworm would die, too.

In commensalism, one organism benefits and the other organism is not affected. Birds called cattle egrets, for example, follow cattle as they move through a field. The birds eat the insects that jump from the grass as the cattle graze. The birds benefit, while the cattle are neither harmed nor helped.

In mutualism, both organisms benefit. Cleaner shrimp, for example, eat parasites off fish. The shrimp get food and the fish stay healthy. This relationship helps both the shrimp and the fish.

 **COMPARE AND CONTRAST** How do the three types of symbiosis compare?

Visual Summary

A natural habitat is the area where an organism lives. It provides everything the organism needs to survive. A niche describes the role of an organism in its habitat.

Adaptations are traits that help organisms survive in their habitats. Adaptations can be physical or behavioral.

Symbiosis is a close, long-lasting relationship between organisms. The three main types of symbiosis are parasitism, commensalism, and mutualism.

LINKS for Home and School

MATH **Make a Line Graph** The table lists the bird population on an island for 4 years. Plot the data on a line graph. Describe the changes you observe.

Year	'00	'01	'02	'03	'04
Pop.	40	92	160	152	148

TECHNOLOGY **Use a Map** Find a topographic map of your state or community. Use the map key to describe the physical features of habitats near you.

Review

1 MAIN IDEA Describe two different niches in a savanna habitat.

2 VOCABULARY Give an example of an adaptation. Describe how the adaptation helps the organism.

3 READING SKILL: Compare and Contrast According to natural selection, how do differences among organisms help develop adaptations?

4 CRITICAL THINKING: Apply How would you describe your niche in your family? How does it compare to an animal's niche in nature?

5 INQUIRY SKILL: Observe Describe a type of symbiotic relationship that you have observed. Identify which organisms benefit and which are harmed, if any.

✓ TEST PREP

An organism's niche includes

A. where it lives.

B. how it protects itself.

C. how it reproduces.

D. all of the above.

 Technology

Visit **www.eduplace.com/scp/** to find out more about habitats and niches.

What Factors Affect Ecosystems?

Why It Matters...

How many wolves can live in a forest? The answer depends on the size of the forest and the amount of food it provides for the wolves. Temperature can affect the population, and so can pollution. In any population—of wolves, trees, birds, or people—the size is limited by the available resources.

PREPARE TO INVESTIGATE

Inquiry Skill

Hypothesize When you hypothesize, you use prior knowledge or observations to suggest a cause-and-effect relationship that can be tested.

Materials

- measuring cup
- 3 plastic cups
- 32 lima bean seeds
- soil
- water
- marker
- safety goggles

Science and Math Toolbox

For step 4, review **Making a Chart to Organize Data** on page H11.

Limits to Growth

Procedure

Safety: Wear goggles while handling soil.

1. **Collaborate** Work with a partner. Label the three cups A, B, and C. Place soil into the cups until they are nearly full. Each cup should contain roughly the same amount of soil.

2. **Use Variables** Place 2 seeds in cup A. Place 10 seeds in cup B. Place 20 seeds in cup C.

3. **Measure** Measure and pour 25 mL of water into each cup.

4. **Record Data** Place all three cups in a sunny spot. In your *Science Notebook,* make a chart like the one shown for each cup.

5. **Observe** Over the course of the next three weeks, water the cups when the soil is dry and measure growth. Be certain that all the cups receive the same amount of water and sunlight. Record the date, height, and your observations at least twice a week.

Conclusion

1. **Observe** What differences did you observe in the growing seeds?

2. **Hypothesize** What factor might have caused these differences?

3. **Use Variables** Why was it important to give each cup the same amount of sunlight and water?

STEP 1

STEP 2

STEP 4

Cup _____

Date	Height	Observations

Investigate More!

Design an Experiment
Design an experiment to determine how sunlight affects plant growth. Remember to keep other variables constant, and to include a control.

VOCABULARY

extinction	p. B51
population	p B46
predator	p. B47
prey	p. B47

READING SKILL

Cause and Effect As you read, look for cause-and-effect relationships in populations and ecosystems.

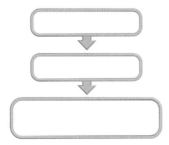

Changes in Population

Main Idea The size of any population can vary over time. It responds to changes in climate and resources.

A Balanced Ecosystem

Different living things use the resources of an ecosystem in different ways. They take some resources from ecosystems and add others to it. A balanced ecosystem has enough resources for all of its living things.

Every ecosystem supports many populations. A **population** is all the organisms of a given species that live together in the same area. Any change in one part of an ecosystem can upset the balance. For example, suppose a fungus kills many of the plants that rabbits eat. Such an event could lower the rabbit population. This would affect the hawks, owls, and other animals that eat the rabbits.

On the other hand, if a population of rabbits becomes too large, they might crowd out other species that live in the area. Because ecosystems have limited resources, they can support only a limited number of living things.

Predators that consume frog eggs help keep the frog population from growing too large.

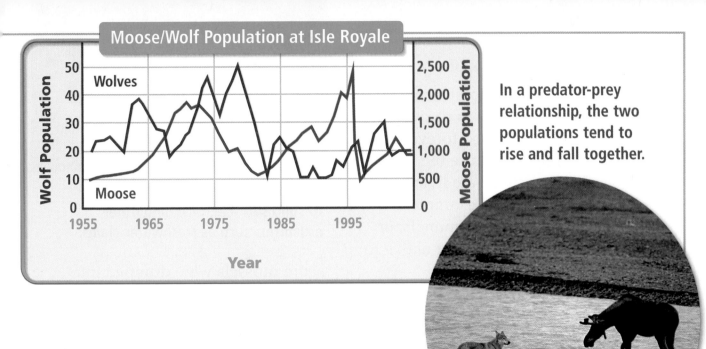

Moose/Wolf Population at Isle Royale

Wolf Population | Moose Population

Year

In a predator-prey relationship, the two populations tend to rise and fall together.

Limits on Populations

In any ecosystem, populations are always changing. Old animals die, and new ones take their place. When a tree falls, plants that thrive in sunlight can begin to grow. Other changes, however, can upset the balance of the ecosystem.

Consider the relationship between predators and their prey. **Predators** are animals that hunt and eat other animals. **Prey** are animals hunted and eaten by predators.

In a healthy ecosystem, the population densities of predators and prey are balanced. But certain factors can upset this balance. One example comes from an actual ecosystem—Isle Royale, an island in Lake Superior.

Moose first appeared on the island around 1900. They may have crossed on ice that formed a temporary bridge from the mainland. The island had plenty of plants for the moose to eat, and no predators.

The population of the moose had skyrocketed by 1930. Then it fell sharply. Why? The moose did not have enough food. Food is a limited resource in an ecosystem. So, the limited food supply on the island helped slow population growth.

In 1950, wolves appeared on the island. Wolves are predators of moose, so the moose population dropped while the wolves increased. Yet after a while, the wolf population dropped because not enough moose remained to support them. With fewer wolves, the moose population rose again. As the graph shows, the populations of these two species continued to rise and fall.

Lack of predators can make an ecosystem unbalanced as prey populations grow unchecked. Adding predators is one way to restore the balance.

▶ **CAUSE AND EFFECT** How might a decrease in predators affect prey?

B47

Changing the Balance

Once changed, an ecosystem may take hundreds of years to recover. In some cases, it is changed forever.

Some factors that cause big changes in ecosystems are living. Alien species are good examples. Alien species are plants, animals, or other organisms that are not native to a given ecosystem.

In some cases, an alien species has no natural predators in its new home. It may thrive and "steal" resources from native plants and animals, or feed directly off them.

How do alien species enter new ecosystems? Often, they are brought in by accident. Zebra mussels, for example, traveled from western Russia to North America during the 1980s in water stored on a boat. The

▲ Zebra mussels anchor themselves to solid surfaces, including other organisms such as freshwater clams.

zebra mussels were dumped into the Great Lakes with the water. By the 1990s, the mussels had spread throughout many lakes and rivers.

The tiny zebra mussels can clog water pipes used by power plants and water treatment facilities. Zebra mussels also harm native organisms. They grow in large groups on clams, mussels, and crayfish. This growth can smother the native species.

Another problem is that zebra mussels filter the water, clearing it of plankton. Plankton are tiny producers. With fewer plankton to eat and to provide oxygen, many native species die.

It can be very difficult to get rid of an alien species. However, many states are working together to control the spread of these troublesome organisms.

◄ The Asian long-horned beetle entered the United States in wooden shipping crates in the 1990s. It burrows under the bark of trees, slowly killing them.

Nonliving things can also change the balance of an ecosystem. These include natural events, such as volcanic eruptions.

For example, Mount St. Helens is a volcano in the state of Washington. For many years, it was like a sleeping giant—it caused no trouble. Hemlock and fir thrived on the mountainside, as did many animals.

Everything changed in May 1980, when the volcano violently erupted. In a matter of minutes, hot lava burned and destroyed trees over an area of 500 square kilometers. Thick deposits of ash covered ground hundreds of kilometers away. The area surrounding the volcano became almost barren.

Within a few years of the Mount St. Helens eruption, flowers bloomed again on nearby slopes.

Yet life slowly returned to the mountain and neighboring areas. Some plants survived the eruption. Wind blew in seeds for grasses and shrubs, which sprouted a year or so after the eruption. Then larger plants moved in, followed by animals that ate those plants.

In 2004, the volcano turned active once again, although the damage was not nearly as severe as before. If the volcano stays quiet for many more years, the forest will return as before.

Other natural events include forest fires, floods, and droughts. Each can cause long-lasting changes in ecosystems. What do you think animals do when ecosystems change?

▶ **CAUSE AND EFFECT** **Describe one way that a nonliving factor may change an ecosystem.**

1983

1980

When a new lizard moved into part of its habitat, the green anole of Florida moved to the treetops. ▲

Adapting to Change

What if your home suddenly lost heat during a cold winter? What would you and your family do? You might move to a new home. Or you might adapt to the cold house, meaning you would find a way to still live there. Maybe you would build a fire or wear warm clothes.

In nature, living things also respond to dramatic changes in their environment. Sometimes they relocate, meaning they move to a new home.

The move need not be far. For example, in recent years a lizard from Cuba invaded part of the Florida habitat of another lizard, the green anole. The green anole used to live close to the ground. When it lost resources to the Cuban lizard, the green anole moved to the treetops.

A living thing can also adapt to changes in its environment. For example, many animals grow thicker coats when the weather turns cold.

If the change is too dramatic, however, the animal might perish, meaning it would die. Perishing is the consequence when living things can neither adapt nor relocate to survive a change.

Living things have relocated, adapted, and perished for as long as they have been on Earth. Fossils give clues to how this happened. Fossils are the remains or traces of once-living things.

Fossils may not show how individual organisms changed, but they do show that different species have lived at different times. Look at the fossil dinosaur shown below. No animal alive today has a skeleton just like this. Because dinosaurs could not survive changes in their environment, they perished.

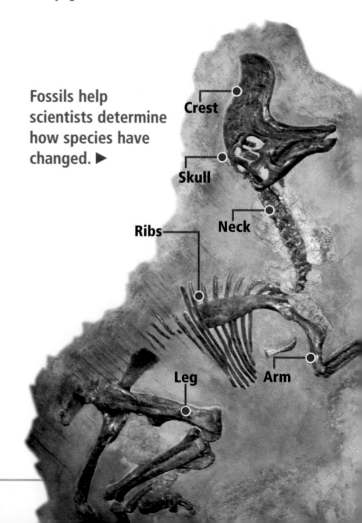

Fossils help scientists determine how species have changed. ▶

Crest

Skull

Neck

Ribs

Leg

Arm

Key

Limestone
Shale
Sandstone
Shale
Conglomerate

Sedimentary rocks form in horizontal layers. Over time, the layers may bend, tilt, or remain flat. ▲

Evidence in Rocks

Change in ecosystems can occur very rapidly and can affect vast areas. For many animals, perishing is often the result. Throughout Earth's history, not only have countless individual organisms perished, but so have entire species.

When this happens, the species becomes extinct. **Extinction** occurs when all members of a species die out. Many different events can cause extinction, even among very successful species.

How do scientists draw conclusions about species that went extinct long ago? They do so by studying both fossils and the rocks in which the fossils were found.

The illustration above, for example, shows layers of rocks from a hillside. These layers formed on top of one another over time. The oldest rocks are on the bottom, the youngest on top. Any fossils in the rocks must have formed at the same time as the rocks around them.

Taken together, fossils and rocks show that species and ecosystems have changed a great deal throughout Earth's history. For example, fossil shells or fish show the land once was underwater. Fossil ferns show a wet, warm climate. Both kinds of fossils have been found in mountains!

Scientists are also able to estimate the age of a fossil, typically through a process called radioactive dating. The oldest fossils are billions of years old.

Sometimes the absence of fossils is key information. For example, Earth's rocks hold a wide variety of dinosaur fossils, yet none in layers younger than 65 million years old. Scientists conclude that all the dinosaurs died at once at this time.

Such an event is called a mass extinction. Earth has experienced several mass extinctions throughout its history.

▶ **CAUSE AND EFFECT** What can scientists learn by studying fossils and rocks?

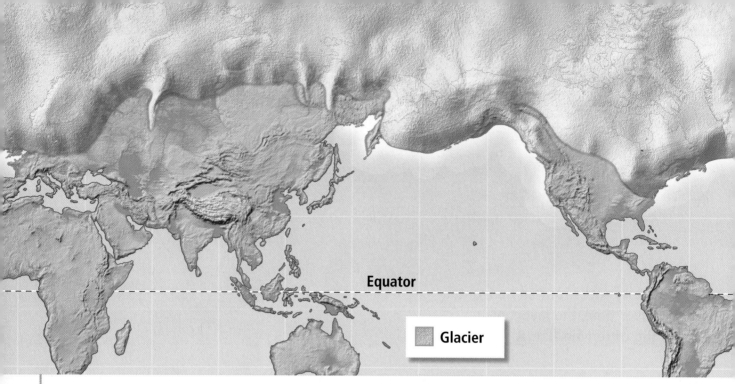

Equator

Glacier

▲ This map shows the extent of the glaciers in the Northern Hemisphere during the most recent ice age, from about 20,000 years ago.

Climate Change

Do you live in New York? Or Minnesota or Michigan? If you could travel back in time—say, 20,000 years—you would not recognize these states. They would be covered under a thick sheet of ice.

Over the last two million years, large parts of North America and Europe have been covered several times by huge ice sheets, or glaciers. These periods are called ice ages. The last ice age ended about 11,000 years ago.

During an ice age, much of Earth's water is locked up in glaciers, causing sea levels to fall. During the last ice age, the drop in sea level exposed a land bridge between Asia and North America. Many living things, humans included, may have crossed this bridge to settle in North America.

Many animals were already in North America at this time. Some were very large, like the woolly mammoth and the saber-toothed cat. With their thick, furry coats, they were well adapted to the cold conditions. When the ice age ended, however, they became extinct.

Some scientists believe that these animals could not adapt to the warmer climate. Other scientists think that both climate and humans caused the extinctions. Humans may have overhunted the great animals.

The exact reasons why some animals became extinct may never be known. But Earth's climate does change periodically. These changes greatly affect the living things upon it.

▶ **CAUSE AND EFFECT** How might climate change affect living things in the future?

Visual Summary

Ecosystems have limited resources. A balanced ecosystem has enough resources to support all living things.

Both living things, such as alien species, and nonliving things, such as volcanic eruptions, can upset the balance of an ecosystem.

Living things can respond to changes in ecosystems by relocating, adapting, or perishing.

LINKS for Home and School

MATH **Calculate Population Density**
Measure the area of your classroom. Determine the number of students in the class. Then calculate the population density of students in the classroom per square meter.

HISTORY **Create a Time Line** Research major mass extinctions that have occurred throughout Earth's history. Make a time line showing when each extinction occurred and what types of organisms were affected.

Review

❶ MAIN IDEA What factors can cause the size of a population of living things to change?

❷ VOCABULARY Use the terms *predator* and *prey* in a sentence.

❸ READING SKILL: Cause and Effect Why do alien species often thrive in their new ecosystems?

❹ CRITICAL THINKING: Apply Does your classroom have unlimited resources? Explain.

❺ INQUIRY SKILL: Hypothesize What changes in living and nonliving things might be brought about by the onset of another ice age?

 TEST PREP
A mass extinction occurs when

A. one animal species dies out.

B. one plant species dies out.

C. many species die out at roughly the same time.

D. many species die out at different times.

 Technology
Visit **www.eduplace.com/scp/** to find out more about populations.

DINOSAUR EXTINCTION

Scientists have dug up dinosaur fossils all over the world. Yet the fossils always are in rock layers older than 65 million years. Younger layers lack them.

What killed the dinosaurs so quickly? Scientists continue to debate this question! Two theories are outlined on the next page.

Whatever killed the dinosaurs also seems to have killed more than half the species of the time—a mass extinction. Earth's climate changed, too. It changed from warm and mild to cool and more varied.

Fortunately, mammals survived the mass extinction. The success of today's mammals—including humans— might stem from this long-ago event.

The asteroid theory of dinosaur extinction was put forth by father-and-son scientists: Luis Alvarez (left) and Walter Alvarez (right). ▼

What killed the dinosaurs?

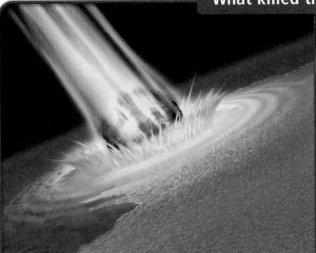

Asteroid Theory

An unusual amount of iridium is found in rock layers from the time of the mass extinction. Iridium metal is rare on Earth's surface, but more common in asteroids. An asteroid strike might have filled the air with dust and debris. If sunlight was blocked, plants would have died, and dinosaurs would have followed.

Volcano Theory

Volcanic eruptions may have filled the air with soot and ash, blocking the Sun. The volcano theory argues that extinction took place more gradually, perhaps over several million years. The theory also explains the iridium deposits, because Earth's interior is high in iridium.

Sharing Ideas

1. **READING CHECK** How do scientists infer that dinosaurs went extinct quickly?

2. **WRITE ABOUT IT** Compare the two theories about the extinction of the dinosaurs.

3. **TALK ABOUT IT** Do you think Earth is in danger of another mass extinction?

How Can Humans Change Ecosytems?

Why It Matters...

Huge numbers of bison once roamed the Great Plains of North America. Yet in the 1800s, humans hunted them almost to extinction. Hunting and other human activities changed not only the bison, but the ecosystems of which they were part.

Changes like this continue today. By understanding how and why ecosystems change, people can manage those changes wisely.

PREPARE TO INVESTIGATE

Inquiry Skill

Predict When you predict, you use observations, facts, or patterns to anticipate results.

Materials

- plastic container with lid
- ice cubes
- modeling clay
- water
- metric ruler

Science and Math Toolbox

For step 2, review **Measurements** on page H16.

Rising Sea Level

Procedure

1. **Use Models** Work with a partner. Use clay to make a model slope inside a shallow plastic container. The slope represents a coastal area. It should be placed at one end of the container.

2. **Measure** Add water to a depth of 2 cm inside the container. The water represents the ocean. It should cover only the edge of the slope.

3. **Predict** Add four ice cubes to the container. The ice cubes represent glaciers. Cover the container. In your *Science Notebook,* predict what will happen to the level of the water when the ice cubes melt.

4. **Record Data** The next day, measure the depth of the water in the container. Record your measurements in a chart.

Conclusion

1. **Observe** What happened to the depth of the water in the container?

2. **Observe** How was the model land affected by the change in the depth of the water?

3. **Predict** How might a rise in sea level affect coastal areas?

Investigate More!

Research Is Earth's average temperature increasing? Research this question. Prepare a report that includes a graph or map to display data.

VOCABULARY

endangered   p. B59
   species
pollution   p. B60
threatened species p. B59

READING SKILL

Draw Conclusions As you read, draw conclusions about the impact of humans on ecosystems.

Tropical rain forests are being cleared for farming and logging. Many species are lost along with the forests. ▼

Human Impact on Ecosystems

Main Idea Human activities impact ecosystems in both positive and negative ways.

Human Activities

Rain forests are among the most valuable resources on Earth. They are home to a vast variety of plants and animals. Yet rain forests are destroyed every day. By one account, almost 200,000 square kilometers (77,000 square miles) are lost each year. That's about 37 city blocks per minute!

People clear rain forests for land to grow crops, raise livestock, and build homes and businesses. Lumber that comes from the trees is valuable, too.

Why should you be concerned about the loss of rain forests? One reason is that plants and animals may become extinct when their habitats are destroyed. Scientists believe that some rain forest plants may contain substances that could be used as medicines. In addition, rain forest plants release oxygen and take in carbon dioxide from the atmosphere.

▲ Developers cut the top off a hillside to build these houses in California.

▲ In the United States alone, more than 4 billion kg (9 billion lbs) of fish are caught each year. Many popular fish are now threatened.

Humans have a huge effect on ecosystems by destroying habitats. In fact, habitat loss is the main reason why rates of extinction are rising. Not only rain forests are affected. Other ecosystems are impacted, too.

Wetlands, for example, are sometimes drained and filled in to provide land for farms, businesses, and housing developments. Until recently, people did not understand the importance of wetlands. These ecosystems help filter harmful chemicals from groundwater.

The spongy grasses in wetland areas also absorb excess water during heavy rains. This action helps reduce flooding. Many animal species hatch in wetlands. Later, as adults, they live in the sea. Wetlands are important nurseries for these animals.

Excessive hunting and fishing practices pose another threat to many ecosystems. In the early 1800s, for example, more than 60 million bison roamed the Great Plains. Yet by 1890, fewer than a thousand were left. Overhunting was the biggest reason. People killed the bison for their hides or tongues.

When a species is close to becoming extinct, it is called an **endangered species.** When a species is close to becoming endangered, it is called a **threatened species.** These categories are important. They let everyone know which species need the most protection.

▶ **DRAW CONCLUSIONS** Is habitat destruction a serious problem? Explain.

B59

Types of Pollution

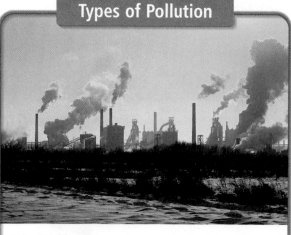

Air Pollution
Factories that burn fossil fuels can release harmful substances into the air.

Water Pollution
Oil spills can harm plants and animals that live in or near the water.

Land Pollution
Trash and garbage are often carelessly discarded, polluting the land.

Pollution

What other human activities can impact ecosystems? Burning fossil fuels is one example. Fossil fuels include oil, gas, and coal. These fuels contain a lot of energy and are easy to use. However, burning them can cause pollution. **Pollution** is the addition of harmful substances to the environment.

When fossil fuels are burned, certain gases and solid particles are released into the air. These pollutants can make the air unhealthy to breathe. Some combine with water droplets to form acids. They fall to the ground as acid rain.

Fossil fuels don't have to be burned to pose a threat to the environment. Oil, for example, is often transported on big ships called tankers. Accidental spills can damage the environment and be expensive to clean. About 300,000 birds died following a major oil spill in Alaska in 1989.

Human activities can also pollute the land. Each year, people in the United States produce hundreds of millions of tons of solid waste, including paper, plastics, and metals. Most solid waste is buried in sanitary landfills, and some is burned. However, people sometimes carelessly dump solid waste along roadsides or in bodies of water.

Some farming and lawn-care practices can also cause pollution. Rain can wash fertilizers into rivers and streams, where they may damage the ecosystem.

Growth of Human Population

Hundreds of years ago, the effects of human activities were relatively small. There were no power plants or motor vehicles. And the human population was much smaller than it is today. As the graph shows, today's human population is very large, and growing larger all the time.

In 1800, only about 1 billion people lived on Earth. By 1930, that number had doubled. A mere 30 years later, the population had increased to 3 billion. Today, more than 6 billion people live on the planet.

Modern humans have been around for thousands of years. Yet our population growth remained fairly steady until the last 200 years. Why has the human population grown so fast in such a short time? Advances in medicine and technology have made it possible for more people to survive diseases and accidents. These same factors help people live longer lives.

Everyone needs food, clean water, clean air, shelter, and other resources. As you've learned, however, ecosystems have limited resources. If the human population continues to grow, not enough resources will be available. In fact, in many parts of the world, food and water are already scarce or poorly managed.

Remember that human activities can harm ecosystems. A growing human population will take up more space. More natural habitats will be lost. More species will be threatened with extinction. Can anything be done to help this situation? Read on to find out how people are protecting the environment.

▶ **DRAW CONCLUSIONS** **How has the growth in human population affected ecosystems around the world?**

A growing human population must compete for a limited amount of resources, such as food, land, and water.

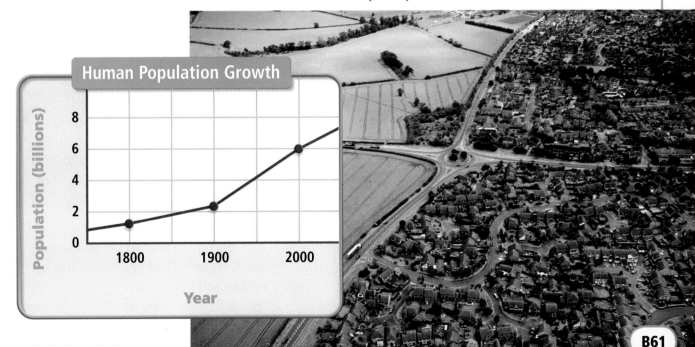

Human Population Growth

Population (billions) vs. Year

Good News

All around the world, people are working to reduce pollution and restore damaged ecosystems. Governments are passing laws. Industries are taking action. And people like you are making a difference everywhere!

▶ **DRAW CONCLUSIONS** How can individual actions help protect the environment?

Wildlife Refuges

In the United States, wildlife refuges cover nearly 40 million hectares (15 million acres). Development and hunting are limited in these refuges.

Cleaner Cars

The Clean Air Act, revised in 1990, limits the pollutants from new cars. Some manufacturers have designed cars that use alternative fuels.

Endangered Species Act

This legislation protects endangered and threatened species from harm by human activities.

Community Actions

Many people work to clean up trash, plant trees, or carpool to school and work. Individuals can make a big difference!

Clean Technology

New technology reduces pollutants at coal-burning power plants.

Protecting Wetlands

The Environmental Protection Agency (EPA) works with state and local governments to protect bogs, swamps, and other wet places.

FLORIDA
07445899
AYE APT
Save the Manatee

Environmental Legislation

Many states have passed laws to protect or support local species. In Florida, funds from license plates help protect manatees.

Visual Summary

Many habitats are destroyed by logging, development, and other human actions. Overharvesting can reduce the populations of certain species.

Pollution affects air, water, and land. A growing human population means that more people are competing for limited resources.

Governments have passed laws to protect the environment. Many industries use new technology to reduce pollution. Individuals can help clean up ecosystems.

LINKS for Home and School

MATH **Make a Table** Read the information about human population on B61 and make a table to show this data. About when was the world population at 4 billion?

WRITE **Explanatory** Use the library or Internet to research how individuals can help the environment. Make a "Help the Environment" booklet. Share the booklet with classmates.

Review

❶ **MAIN IDEA** What are some ways that people affect ecosystems?

❷ **VOCABULARY** What can happen to a threatened species if its population continues to decrease?

❸ **READING SKILL: Draw Conclusions** Can the actions of one person help the environment? Explain your answer.

❹ **CRITICAL THINKING: Synthesis** A plant in a tropical rain forest becomes extinct. Why should this concern you?

❺ **INQUIRY SKILL: Predict** How will Earth's resources be affected if the human population continues to grow?

✓ **TEST PREP**

During the past 200 years, the human population has

A. decreased.

B. stayed the same.

C. increased slightly.

D. increased greatly.

 Technology
Visit **www.eduplace.com/scp/** to find out more about pollution.

Entomologist

Between 7,000 and 10,000 new species of insects are discovered every year! Entomologists study insects to learn how they behave, function, and relate to other organisms in different ecosystems.

Entomology is important for many reasons. Insects recycle nutrients, pollinate crops, and provide food for larger animals. Other insects threaten food supplies or spread diseases.

What It Takes!

- A degree in entomology or biology
- An interest in insects and their environments

Ship's Captain

Boats and ships are visitors to water ecosystems. Sometimes their visits can cause great changes. Fishing boats, oil tankers, and even passenger liners can damage ecosystems if they are not run properly.

A ship's captain needs to understand the ship and its cargo, as well as the environment through which they travel. The job comes with great responsibility.

What It Takes!

- An understanding of sea-going vessels and ocean navigation
- Leadership and management skills

EXTREME Science

Fastest Claw in the West

Wham! What a punch! Call it a shrimp, but for its size, it's the hardest hitter on Earth. The mantis shrimp socks a punch that approaches the force of a bullet! It can smash through the armor of the toughest prey in the blink of an eye.

In an aquarium, a mantis shrimp can spell trouble for the ecosystem. Why? It rapidly shatters and eats all the snails and other shelled creatures in the tank. And good luck getting rid of this powerful puncher! The mantis shrimp is smart. It knows how to hide and strike out from behind cover. It can easily break a person's finger—or even the tough safety glass of a public aquarium.

Sock it to 'em!
A human boxer is no match for the mantis shrimp. In the blink of an eye, the shrimp's club-shaped front leg can reach 50 mph. That's two or three times faster than the fastest human puncher!

Vocabulary

Complete each sentence with a term from the list.

1. A(n) ____ is the area where an organism lives.

2. When a species is very close to becoming extinct, it is called a(n) ____.

3. Predators hunt and eat ____.

4. ____ is the number of living things of a certain species in a given area.

5. A(n) ____ is an organism's role in its habitat.

6. Burning fossil fuels and dumping trash can cause ____.

7. A lion is an example of a(n) ____ that hunts zebras.

8. The flippers on a sea turtle are an example of a physical ____.

9. ____ occurs when all the members of a certain species die off.

10. Parasitism, commensalism, and mutualism are types of ____.

adaptation B40
endangered species B59
extinction B51
habitat B38
niche B39
pollution B60
population B46
predator B47
prey B47
symbiosis B42
threatened species B59

Test Prep

Write the letter of the best answer choice.

11. What best describes a species that would be classified as endangered if it lost more members?

   A. extinct
   B. thriving
   C. alien
   D. threatened

12. Potentially harmful organisms that are not native to a given ecosystem are called ____.

   A. predators
   B. alien species
   C. parasites
   D. threatened species

13. In the process of ____, organisms that are best suited to their environments survive and pass on their traits to their offspring.

   A. natural selection
   B. mass extinction
   C. niches and habitats
   D. behavioral adaptation

14. Which of the following is NOT a way that humans affect ecosystems?

   A. pollution
   B. development
   C. earthquakes
   D. overharvesting

15. Observe Look around the area in which you live for examples of how humans have changed local ecosystems. Write a short paragraph describing these changes.

16. Predict A fire destroyed a forest. After a year, grasses began to grow back in the area. Soon after that, rabbits moved in to eat the grass. The rabbits had no major predators, so their population grew. Recently, foxes and hawks returned to the area. Predict how the population of the rabbits will change.

Map the Concept

Fill in the concept map by writing definitions for each term.

Critical Thinking

17. Synthesizing What might be done to stop the spread of harmful alien species? List three ideas and discuss why they could work.

18. Applying What are some things you can do to help the environment? How could you encourage people to join you?

19. Evaluating Is it helpful to classify organisms as endangered or threatened? Why or why not?

20. Analyzing Humans, other mammals, and birds can maintain a constant body temperature. Why is this a useful adaptation? How does this explain the spread of these animals around Earth?

Performance Assessment

Make a Fossil

Use clay to make a model fossil. Select an object such as a leaf and press it into the clay. Or, trace the outline of an animal's footprint in the clay. Exchange your model with another student. What can you infer about the plant or animal from studying the fossil?

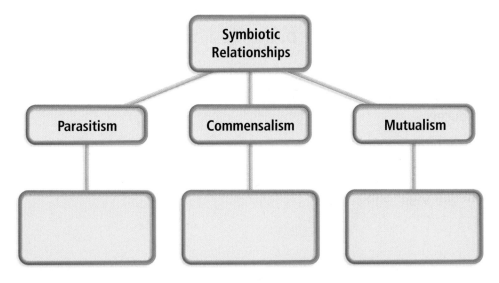

Write the letter of the best answer choice.

1. A hookworm lives by using the nutrients in a dog's digestive system. Which type of symbiosis is this?

hookworm

   A. commensalism

   B. mutualism

   C. organism

   D. parasitism

2. Which is the second-level consumer in this food chain?

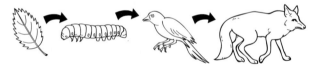

   A. bird

   B. caterpillar

   C. fox

   D. leaf

3. Which is NOT a reason that rain forests should be preserved?

   A. They contain many producers.

   B. They are home to many habitats.

   C. They are good for growing crops.

   D. They contain many different organisms.

4. Which factor is MOST important in creating the difference in biomes?

   A. physical features

   B. temperature

   C. plant life

   D. climate

5. Which is Earth's largest land biome?

   A. desert

   B. grasslands

   C. tundra

   D. taiga

6. The marine organism shown lives in the _____ .

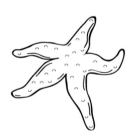

   A. shore zone.

   B. intertidal zone.

   C. near-shore zone.

   D. open ocean zone.

7. The illustration below shows part of a forest ecosystem. Which is part of the ecosystem but not part of the forest community?

A. rock

B. grass

C. mouse

D. bird

8. The illustration below is MOST likely a
_____ .

A. taiga biome.

B. tundra biome.

C. desert biome.

D. grassland biome.

Answer the following in complete sentences.

9. What is a mass extinction? Give two examples of what might cause a mass extinction.

10. Explain what an alien species is and how the introduction of an alien species can affect ecosystems.

Discover!

Grasslands can be hot and dry in the summer, with temperatures sometimes climbing over 38°C (100°F). Animals that live in hot places must find a way to keep cool. The jackrabbit's long ears are adapted not only for hearing, but to help cool its body.

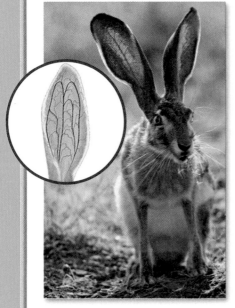

A jackrabbit's ears are about 20 cm long. The wind cools the ear's thin skin, which cools blood vessels lying closely beneath.

Other kinds of rabbits cannot survive high temperatures. They would suffer fatal heat strokes at temperatures of around 25°C (77°F) or higher.

Snowshoe hares live in cold, Arctic climates. Small ears help trap body heat inside.

All organisms have adaptations to help them survive in their natural habitats. Adaptations include physical features, such as ear shape and length, as well as behaviors, such as feeding at night instead of the day. Many organisms are adapted to very specific habitats. If their habitat is destroyed, they may not survive elsewhere.

Learn more about adaptations. Go to **www.eduplace.com/scp/** for examples of other adaptations that help animals and plants survive.

Science and Math Toolbox

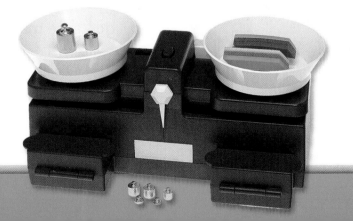

Using a Microscope

A microscope makes it possible to see very small things by magnifying them. Some microscopes have a set of lenses that magnify objects by different amounts.

Examine Some Salt Grains

Handle a microscope carefully; it can break easily. Carry it firmly with both hands and avoid touching the lenses.

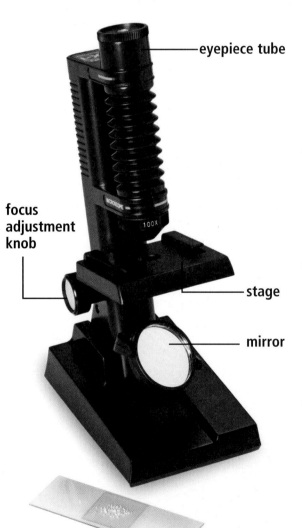

eyepiece tube

focus adjustment knob

100X

stage

mirror

microscope slide

1 Turn the mirror toward a source of light. **NEVER** use the Sun as a light source.

2 Place a few grains of salt on the slide. Put the slide on the stage of the microscope.

3 Bring the salt grains into focus. Turn the adjustment knob on the back of the microscope as you look through the eyepiece.

4 Raise the eyepiece tube to increase the magnification; lower it to decrease magnification.

Making a Bar Graph

A bar graph helps you organize and compare data. For example, you might want to make a bar graph to compare weather data for different places.

Make a Bar Graph of Annual Snowfall

For more than 20 years, the cities listed in the table have been recording their yearly snowfall. The table shows the average number of centimeters of snow that the cities receive each year. Use the data in the table to make a bar graph showing the cities' average annual snowfall.

Snowfall	
City	Snowfall (cm)
Atlanta, GA	5
Charleston, SC	1.5
Houston, TX	1
Jackson, MS	3
New Orleans, LA	0.5
Tucson, AZ	3

1. **Title your graph.** The title should help a reader understand what your graph describes.

2. **Choose a scale and mark equal intervals.** The vertical scale should include the least value and the greatest value in the set of data.

3. **Label the vertical axis** *Snowfall (cm)* and the horizontal axis *City*. Space the city names equally.

4. **Carefully graph the data.** Depending on the interval you choose, some amounts may be between two numbers.

5. **Check each step of your work.**

Average Annual Snowfall of Selected Cities

Using a Calculator

After you've made measurements, a calculator can help you analyze your data. Some calculators have a memory key that allows you to save the result of one calculation while you do another.

Add and Divide to Find Percent

The table shows the amount of rain that was collected using a rain gauge in each month of one year. You can use a calculator to help you find the total yearly rainfall. Then you can find the percent of rain that fell during January.

Rainfall	
Month	**Rain (mm)**
Jan.	214
Feb.	138
Mar.	98
Apr.	157
May	84
June	41
July	5
Aug.	23
Sept.	48
Oct.	75
Nov.	140
Dec.	108

1 Add the numbers. When you add a series of numbers, you need not press the equal sign until the last number is entered. Just press the plus sign after you enter each number (except the last).

2 If you make a mistake while you are entering numbers, press the clear entry (CE/C) key to erase your mistake. Then you can continue entering the rest of the numbers you are adding. If you can't fix your mistake, you can press the (CE/C) key once or twice until the screen shows 0. Then start over.

3 Your total should be 1,131. Now clear the calculator until the screen shows 0. Then divide the rainfall amount for January by the total yearly rainfall (1,131). Press the percent (%) key. Then press the equal sign key.

214 [÷] 1131 [%] [=]

The percent of yearly rainfall that fell in January is 18.921309, which rounds to 19%.

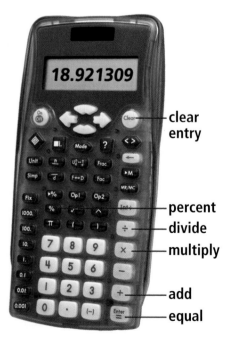

clear entry

percent

divide

multiply

add

equal

Finding an Average

An average is a way to describe a set of data using one number. For example, you could compare the surface temperature of several stars that are of the same type. You could find the average surface temperature of these stars.

Add and Divide to Find the Average

Suppose scientists found the surface temperature of eight blue-white stars to be those shown in the table. What is the average surface temperature of the stars listed?

1 First find the sum of the data. Add the numbers in the list.

```
    7,200
    6,100
    6,000
    6,550
    7,350
    6,800
    7,500
 +  6,300
  ───────
   53,800
```

2 Then divide the sum (53,800) by the number of addends (8).

```
         6,725
     8 ) 53,800
       − 48
       ────
         58
       − 56
       ────
         20
       − 16
       ────
         40
       − 40
       ────
          0
```

3 53,800 ÷ 8 = 6,725
The average surface temperature of these eight blue-white stars is 6,725°F.

Using a Tape Measure or Ruler

Tape measures, metersticks, and rulers are tools for measuring length. Scientists use units such as kilometers, meters, centimeters, and millimeters when making length measurements.

Use a Meterstick

1 Work with a partner to find the height of your reach. Stand facing a chalkboard. Reach up as high as you can with one hand.

2 Have your partner use chalk to mark the chalkboard at the highest point of your reach.

3 Use a meterstick to measure your reach to the nearest centimeter. Measure from the floor to the chalk mark. Record the height.

Use a Tape Measure

1 Use a tape measure to find the circumference of, or distance around, your partner's head. Wrap the tape around your partner's head.

2 Find the line where the tape begins to wrap over itself.

3 Record the distance around your partner's head to the nearest millimeter.

Measuring Volume

A graduated cylinder, a measuring cup, and a beaker are used to measure volume. Volume is the amount of space something takes up. Most of the containers that scientists use to measure volume have a scale marked in milliliters (mL).

▲ This measuring cup has marks for every 25 mL.

▲ This beaker has marks for every 50 mL.

▲ This graduated cylinder has marks for every 1 mL.

Measure the Volume of a Liquid

1. Measure the volume of some juice. Pour the juice into a measuring container.

2. Move your head so that your eyes are level with the top of the juice. Read the scale line that is closest to the surface of the juice. If the surface of the juice is curved up on the sides, look at the lowest point of the curve.

3. Read the measurement on the scale. You can estimate the value between two lines on the scale to obtain a more accurate measurement.

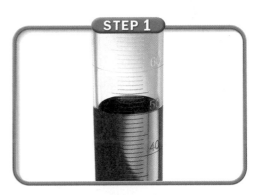

STEP 1

STEP 3

The bottom of the curve is at 50 mL.

Using a Thermometer

A thermometer is used to measure temperature. When the liquid in the tube of a thermometer gets warmer, it expands and moves farther up the tube. Different scales can be used to measure temperature, but scientists usually use the Celsius scale.

Measure the Temperature of a Liquid

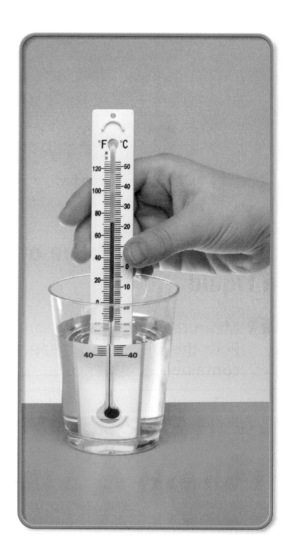

1 Half fill a cup with water or another liquid.

2 Hold the thermometer so that the bulb is in the center of the liquid. Be sure that there are no bright lights or direct sunlight shining on the bulb.

3 Wait until you see the liquid in the tube of the thermometer stop moving. Read the scale line that is closest to the top of the liquid in the tube. The thermometer shown reads 22°C (about 71°F).

Using a Balance

A balance is used to measure mass. Mass is the amount of matter in an object. To find the mass of an object, place the object in the left pan of the balance. Place standard masses in the right pan.

Measure the Mass of a Ball

1. Check that the empty pans are balanced, or level with each other. When balanced, the pointer on the base should be on the middle mark. If it needs to be adjusted, move the slider on the back of the balance a little to the left or right.

2. Place a ball in the left pan. Then add standard masses, one at a time, to the right pan. When the pointer is at the middle mark again, each pan is holding the same amount of matter, and the same mass.

3. Each standard mass is marked to show its number of grams. Add the number of grams marked on the masses in the pan. The total is the mass of the ball in grams.

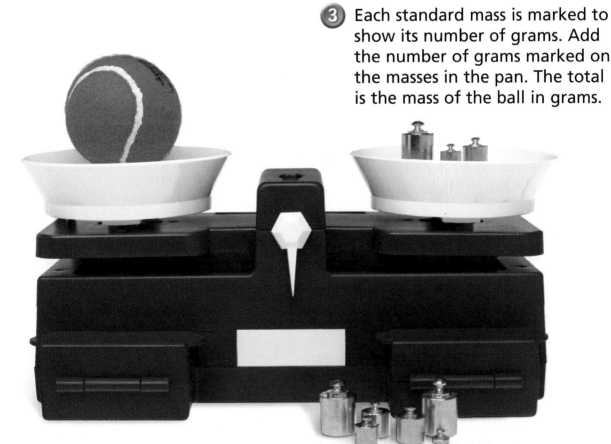

Using an Equation or Formula

Equations and formulas can help you to determine measurements that are not easily made.

Use the Diameter of a Circle to Find Its Circumference

1 Find the circumference of a circle that has a diameter of 10 cm. To determine the circumference of a circle, use the formula below.

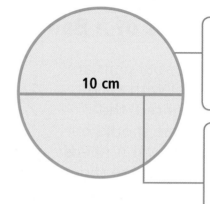

10 cm

The circumference (C) is a measure of the distance around a circle.

The diameter (d) of a circle is a line segment that passes through the center of the circle and connects two points on the circle.

$C = \pi d$

$C = 3.14 \times 10$ cm

$C = 31.4$ cm

The circumference of this circle is 31.4 cm.

π is the symbol for pi. Always use 3.14 as the value for π, unless another value for pi is given.

Use Rate and Time to Determine Distance

2 Suppose an aircraft travels at 772 km/h for 2.5 hours. How many kilometers does the aircraft travel during that time? To determine distance traveled, use the distance formula below.

d = distance

r = rate, or the speed at which the aircraft is traveling.

t = the length of time traveled

$d = rt$

$d = 772 \times 2.5$ km

$d = 1,930$ km

The aircraft travels 1,930 km in 2.5 hours.

Making a Chart to Organize Data

A chart can help you record, compare, or classify information.

Organize Properties of Elements

Suppose you collected the data shown at the right. The data presents properties of silver, gold, lead, and iron.

You could organize this information in a chart by classifying the physical properties of each element.

My Data

Silver (Ag) has a density of 10.5 g/cm^3. It melts at 961°C and boils at 2,212°C. It is used in dentistry and to make jewelry and electronic conductors.

Gold melts at 1,064°C and boils at 2,966°C. Its chemical symbol is Au. It has a density of 19.3 g/cm^3 and is used for jewelry, in coins, and in dentistry.

The melting point of lead (Pb) is 328°C. The boiling point is 1,740°C. It has a density of 11.3 g/cm^3. Some uses for lead are in storage batteries, paints, and dyes.

Iron (Fe) has a density of 7.9 g/cm^3. It will melt at 1,535°C and boil at 3,000°C. It is used for building materials, in manufacturing, and as a dietary supplement.

Create categories that describe the information you have found.

Give the chart a title that describes what is listed in it.

Make sure the information is listed accurately in each column.

Properties of Some Elements

Element	Symbol	Density g/cm^3	Melting Point (°C)	Boiling Point (°C)	Some Uses
Silver	Ag	10.5	961	2,212	jewelry, dentistry, electric conductors
Gold	Au	19.3	1,064	2,966	jewelry, dentistry, coins
Lead	Pb	11.3	328	1,740	storage batteries, paints, dyes
Iron	Fe	7.9	1,535	3,000	building materials, manufacturing, dietary supplement

Reading a Circle Graph

A circle graph shows the whole divided into parts. You can use a circle graph to compare parts to each other or to compare parts to the whole.

Read a Circle Graph of Land Area

The whole circle represents the approximate land area of all of the continents on Earth. The number on each wedge indicates the land area of each continent. From the graph you can determine that the land area of North America is 16% × 148,000,000 km², or about 24 million square kilometers.

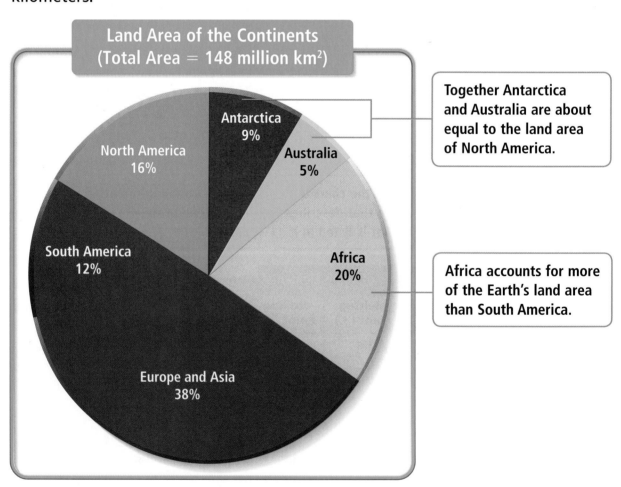

Land Area of the Continents (Total Area = 148 million km²)

Antarctica 9%
Australia 5%
North America 16%
Africa 20%
South America 12%
Europe and Asia 38%

Together Antarctica and Australia are about equal to the land area of North America.

Africa accounts for more of the Earth's land area than South America.

Making a Line Graph

A line graph is a way to show continuous change over time. You can use the information from a table to make a line graph.

Make a Line Graph of Temperatures

The table shows temperature readings over a 12-hour period at the Dallas-Fort Worth Airport in Texas. This data can also be displayed in a line graph that shows temperature change over time.

Dallas-Fort Worth Airport Temperature	
Hour	Temp. (°C)
6 A.M.	22
7 A.M.	24
8 A.M.	25
9 A.M.	26
10 A.M.	27
11 A.M.	29
12 noon	31
1 P.M.	32
2 P.M.	33
3 P.M.	34
4 P.M.	35
5 P.M.	35
6 P.M.	34

1. Choose a title. The title should help a reader understand what your graph describes.

2. Choose a scale and mark equal intervals. The vertical scale should include the least value and the greatest value in the set of data.

3. Label the horizontal axis *Time* and the vertical axis *Temperature* (°C).

4. Write the hours on the horizontal axis. Space the hours equally.

5. Carefully graph the data. Depending on the interval you choose, some temperatures will be between two numbers.

6. Check each step of your work.

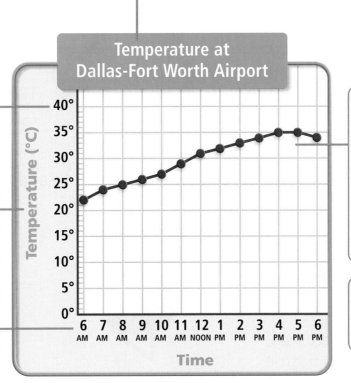

Temperature at Dallas-Fort Worth Airport

Measuring Elapsed Time

Sometimes you may need to find out how much time has passed, or elapsed. A clock is often used to find elapsed time. You can also change units and add or subtract to find out how much time has passed.

Using a Clock to Find Elapsed Minutes

You need to time an experiment for 20 minutes. It is 1:30.

- Start at 1:30.

- Count ahead 20 minutes, by fives to 1:50.

- Stop the experiment at 1:50.

Using a Clock or Stopwatch to Find Elapsed Seconds

You need to time an experiment for 15 seconds. You can use a second hand on a clock.

1. Wait until the second hand is on a number. Then start the experiment.

2. Stop the experiment when 15 seconds have passed.

You can also use a stopwatch to figure out elapsed seconds.

1. Press the reset button on the stopwatch so you see 0:00₀₀.

2. Press the start button to begin.

3. When you see 0:15₀₀, press the stop button on the watch.

Changing Units and Then Adding or Subtracting to Find Elapsed Time

If you know how to change units of time, you can use addition and subtraction to find elapsed time.

1 To change from a larger unit to a smaller unit, multiply.

2 d = ■ h

2 × 24 = 48

2 d = 48 h

2 To change from a smaller unit to a larger unit, divide.

78 wk = ■ yr

$78 ÷ 52 = 1\frac{1}{2}$

$78 \text{ wk} = 1\frac{1}{2} \text{ yr}$

Another Example

Suppose it took juice in an ice-pop mold from 6:40 A.M. until 10:15 A.M. to freeze. How long did it take for the juice to freeze? To find out, subtract.

9 h	75 min
~~10 h~~	~~15 min~~
− 6 h	40 min
3 h	35 min

Rename 10 hr 15 min as 9 h 75 min, since 1 hr = 60 min.

You can also add to find elapsed time.

3 h	30 min	14 s
+ 1 h	40 min	45 s
4 h	70 min	59 s = 5 h 10 min 59 s

Units of Time

60 seconds (s) = 1 minute (min)

60 minutes = 1 hour (hr)

24 hours = 1 day (d)

7 days = 1 week (wk)

52 weeks = 1 year (yr)

Measurements

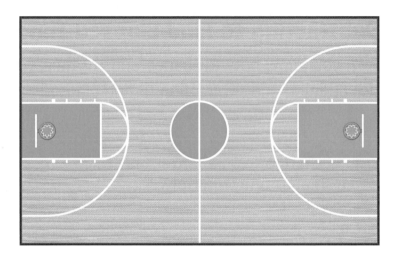

Volume

1 L of sports drink is a little more than 1 qt.

Area

A basketball court covers about 4,700 ft². It covers about 435 m².

Metric Measures

Temperature

- Ice melts at 0 degrees Celsius (°C)
- Water freezes at 0°C
- Water boils at 100°C

Length and Distance

- 1,000 meters (m) = 1 kilometer (km)
- 100 centimeters (cm) = 1 m
- 10 millimeters (mm) = 1 cm

Force

- 1 newton (N) =
  1 kilogram × 1 (meter/second) per second

Volume

- 1 cubic meter (m³) = 1 m × 1 m × 1 m
- 1 cubic centimeter (cm³) =
  1 cm × 1 cm × 1 cm
- 1 liter (L) = 1,000 milliliters (mL)
- 1 cm³ = 1 mL

Area

- 1 square kilometer (km²) = 1 km × 1 km
- 1 hectare = 10,000 m²

Mass

- 1,000 grams (g) = 1 kilogram (kg)
- 1,000 milligrams (mg) = 1 g

Temperature

The temperature at an indoor basketball game might be 27°C, which is 80°F.

Length/Distance

A basketball rim is about 10 ft high, or a little more than 3 m from the floor.

Customary Measures

Temperature

- Ice melts at 32 degrees Fahrenheit (°F)
- Water freezes at 32°F
- Water boils at 212°F

Length and Distance

- 12 inches (in.) = 1 foot (ft)
- 3 ft = 1 yard (yd)
- 5,280 ft = 1 mile (mi)

Weight

- 16 ounces (oz) = 1 pound (lb)
- 2,000 pounds = 1 ton (T)

Volume of Fluids

- 8 fluid ounces (fl oz) = 1 cup (c)
- 2 c = 1 pint (pt)
- 2 pt = 1 quart (qt)
- 4 qt = 1 gallon (gal)

Metric and Customary Rates

- km/h = kilometers per hour
- m/s = meters per second
- mph = miles per hour

Health and Fitness Handbook

Who is in charge of your health? You! Doctors, nurses, your parents or guardian, and teachers can all help you stay healthy. However, it's up to you to make healthful choices. What are some healthful choices you can make? In this section you'll learn:

- how to keep your body systems strong and healthy
- how to choose healthful foods
- how to exercise your heart and lungs every day
- how to be prepared for emergencies
- the benefits of avoiding alcohol, tobacco, and other drugs

The Muscular System

Your muscular system has three types of muscles.

- *Skeletal muscles* pull on bones to move them. You use them whenever you move your body.

- *Cardiac muscles* make up the walls of your heart and keep it beating.

- *Smooth muscles* line the blood vessels, the stomach, and other organs.

Most skeletal muscles are *voluntary muscles.* You can control them. Cardiac and smooth muscles are *involuntary muscles.* They work without you even having to think about them!

Many skeletal muscles work in pairs. When the biceps muscle in your arm contracts (gets shorter), the triceps muscle relaxes (gets longer). As a result, the elbow bends. How would the muscles work together to straighten the arm?

FACTS

- Your muscles receive about 50 messages from your brain every second.

- You have more than 650 muscles.

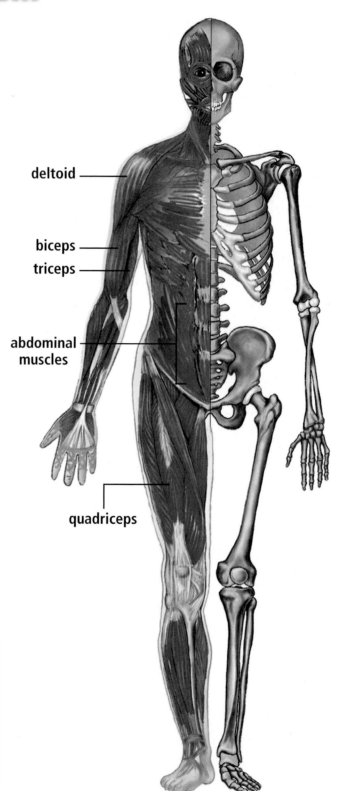

deltoid

biceps

triceps

abdominal muscles

quadriceps

The Skeletal System

Joints connect bones. If you had no joints, you could not bend or move. Each type of joint allows different kinds of movement. Your elbow has a hinge joint. The arm bends only one way at the elbow. Think about your shoulder. It has a ball-and-socket joint. What movement does it allow?

Your skeletal system gives your body strength and support. It works with your muscular system to move body parts. Your bones also protect your organs.

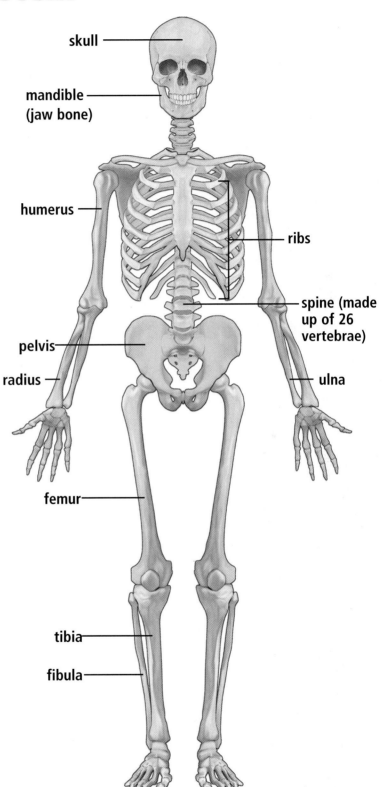

- skull
- mandible (jaw bone)
- humerus
- ribs
- spine (made up of 26 vertebrae)
- pelvis
- radius
- ulna
- femur
- tibia
- fibula

FACTS

- You have 206 bones in your body. More than half of them are found in your hands and feet!

- Your bones come in all shapes and sizes. There's even a bone in your ear shaped like a hammer!

Exercise Your Heart and Lungs

Exercise that makes your heart and lungs work hard is called aerobic exercise. *Aerobic* means "with oxygen." Any kind of steady exercise that raises your heart and breathing rates is aerobic exercise. Jogging, swimming, bicycling, and playing soccer are all good ways to get aerobic exercise.

Five steps toward a great aerobic workout.

1. **Choose your activity.** Pick an activity you enjoy. Do you like exercising with others? Basketball might be a good choice. Do you like exercising to music? Maybe you'd like dancing!

2. **Get the equipment you need.** Make sure you have the right clothes and shoes for your activity. Wear any safety gear you need. Your clothes and safety gear should fit correctly. Ask a parent, guardian, or physical education teacher for help.

3. **Warm up.** Do gentle activity such as walking for five minutes. Then stretch your muscles.

4. **Exercise.** It's best to exercise for at least 20 minutes. Exercise at a level that makes your heart and lungs work. Stop right away if you are injured.

5. **Cool down.** Exercise at a lower level for five to ten minutes to let your heart and breathing rates come back down. Then stretch your muscles again.

Food Labels

The United States Food and Drug Administration (FDA) requires most companies that sell food to label their packages. The facts shown on food labels can help you make smart food choices. Food labels list the ingredients in the food. They are in order by weight. This means that the food contains the most of the first ingredient listed. The label also tells you the name of the company that makes the food and the total weight or volume of the food in the package.

Food labels also include the Nutrition Facts panel. The panel on the right is for a can of chicken soup.

Nutrition Facts
Serving Size 1 cup (246g)
Servings Per Container About 2

Amount Per Serving

Calories 110	Calories from Fat 20

	% Daily Value*
Total Fat 2.5g	4%
Saturated Fat 0.5g	3%
Cholesterol 25mg	8%
Sodium 960mg	40%
Total Carbohydrate 15g	5%
Dietary Fiber 1g	5%
Sugars 2g	
Protein 9g	

Vitamin A 30%	•	Vitamin C 0%
Calcium 2%	•	Iron 4%

*Percent Daily Values are based on a 2,000 calorie diet.

▲ What nutrients are in the food you eat? Read the Nutrition Facts panel to find out! Calories measure the energy in food.

FACTS

Get Enough Nutrients

- Carbohydrates provide energy. Fiber helps the digestive system.
- Your body uses protein for growth and development.
- Vitamins and minerals are important for many body functions.

FACTS

Limit Some Nutrients

- A healthful diet includes a limited amount of fat. Saturated fats and trans fats can increase the risk of heart disease. Cholesterol is a fat-like substance that can clog arteries.
- Too much sodium can increase the risk of high blood pressure.

Emergency Safety

Earthquakes, hurricanes, and tornadoes are all examples of natural disasters. You can plan ahead so you know what to do when a disaster happens.

Plan Ahead

You might not have fresh running water or electricity during a natural disaster. Here are some items you might want to have on hand.

- flashlights with batteries
- candles or lanterns with matches
- at least two gallons of fresh water
- canned or packaged food that does not need to be cooked
- radio with batteries
- first-aid kit

What To Do

Earthquake Get under something solid like a desk or doorway. Stay away from windows. Also stay away from anything that might fall on you. If you are outdoors, get to a wide open area.

Hurricane If there is some warning that a hurricane is coming, you may be told to evacuate. Tape all windows. Your parents or guardian will probably shut off the gas, water, and electricity.

Tornado If you are inside, go to a storm shelter or basement if you can. If there is no basement, go to an inside room with no windows. If you are outside, lie down in a low area and cover your head.

Tobacco, Alcohol, and Other Drugs

A drug is any substance, other than food, that changes how the body works. Drugs are swallowed, smoked, inhaled, or injected.

Helpful Drugs

Some drugs are helpful. Medicines can treat diseases and relieve pain. Drugs people can buy without a doctor's order are called *over-the-counter medicines.* Medicines that need a doctor's order are called *prescription medicines.*

Medicines can harm you if you use them incorrectly. Only take medicine when your parent, guardian, or doctor tells you to. Follow your doctor's instructions or the instructions printed on the package.

Harmful Drugs

Some drugs can harm your health.

Tobacco is a leaf that is smoked, sniffed, or chewed. Tobacco contains many harmful substances, including nicotine which speeds up the heart. Tobacco is addictive. This means that it is very hard to stop using tobacco once a person starts. Tobacco increases your risk of heart disease and lung disease.

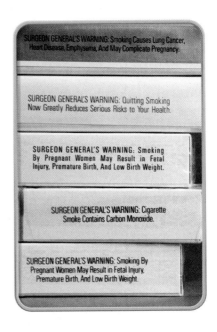

Alcohol is a drug found in drinks such as beer and wine. Alcohol slows brain activity and muscle activity. Heavy drinking can lead to addiction and can damage the liver and other organs. People who drink alcohol are more likely to get into accidents.

Illegal drugs include marijuana, cocaine, ecstasy, LSD, and amphetamines. These drugs can cause serious physical, emotional, and social problems.

Glossary

acceleration (ak sehl uh RAY shuhn), change in velocity (F9)

acquired trait (uh KWYRD trayt), characteristic that an organism develops after it is born (A84)

adaptation (ad ap TAY shuhn), a trait or characteristic that helps an organism survive in its environment (A102, B40)

air mass (air mas), huge volume of air responsible for types of weather (D18)

analyze data (AN uh lyz DAY tuh), to look for patterns in collected information that lead to making logical inferences, predictions, and hypotheses

angiosperms (AN jee uh spurmz), plants with seeds covered by protective fruits (A70)

asexual reproduction (ay SEHK shoo uhl ree pruh DUHK shuhn), production of offspring from only one parent (A96)

ask questions (ask KWEHS chunz), to state questions orally or in writing to find out how or why something happens

asteroid (AS tuh royd), small, rocky object that orbits the Sun (D58)

atmosphere (AT muh sfihr), mixture of gases that surrounds Earth (D16)

atom (AT uhm), the smallest particle of an element that still has the properties of that element (E6)

autumnal equinox (aw TUHM nuhl EE kwuh nahks), September 22 or 23, when the number of hours of daylight and darkness are the same (D34)

axis (AK sihs), imaginary line that goes through the center of Earth from the North Pole to the South Pole (D32)

biome (BY ohm), large group of similar ecosystems (B12)

boiling point (BOY lihng point), temperature at which a substance changes from a liquid to a gas (E45)

cell (sehl), the basic structural unit of a living thing (A6)

chemical change (KEHM ih kuhl chaynj), change in matter that results in new substances being formed (E53)

chemical formula (KEHM ih kuhl FAWR myuh luh), a shorthand way to describe the chemical makeup of a compound (E29)

chemical property (KEHM ih kuhl PRAHP uhr tee), ability of a material to change its chemical makeup (E43)

chemical reaction (KEHM ih kuhl ree AK shuhn), a process in which one or more substances are changed into one or more different substances, or a specific example of one or more chemical changes (E28, E53)

chemical symbol (KEHM ih kuhl SIHM buhl), a letter or letters that abbreviates an element's name (E16)

chlorophyll (KLAWR uh fihl), the green pigment in leaves that collects energy from sunlight (A51)

chloroplasts (KLAWR uh plastz), plant organelles inside which photosynthesis takes place (A51)

chromosome (KROH muh sohm), short, thick coil of DNA (A86)

cilia (SIHL ee uh), small structures that look like hairs (A16)

classification (klas uh fih KAY shuhn), process of sorting things based on similarities and differences (A24)

classify (KLAS uh fy), to sort objects into groups according to their properties to order objects according to a pattern

climate (KLY miht), normal pattern of weather that occurs in an area over a long period of time (B12, D7)

collaborate (kuh LAB uh rayt), to work as a team with others to collect and share data, observations, findings, and ideas

comet (KAHM iht), small orbiting body made of dust, ice, and frozen gases (D59)

communicate (kah MYOO nuh kayt), to explain procedures or share information, data, or findings with others through written or spoken words, actions, graphs, charts, tables, diagrams, or sketches

community (kuh MYOO nih tee), group of living things of different species found in an ecosystem (B7)

compare (kuhm PAIR), to observe and tell how objects or events are alike or different

compound (KAHM pownd), a substance that is made up of two or more elements that are chemically combined (E26)

condensation (kahn dehn SAY shuhn), change of state from a gas to a liquid as energy is removed (E85)

conduction (kuhn DUHK shuhn), transfer of thermal energy between two substances or between two parts of the same substance (F88)

conductivity (kuhn duhk TIHV ih tee), ability to carry energy (E46)

conductor (kuhn DUHK tuhr), material that easily transfers thermal energy or electricity (F92)

conservation (kahn sur VAY shuhn), efficient use of resources (C78)

consumer (kuhn SOO muhr), organism that gets energy by eating food, not producing it (B24)

contour lines (KAHN tur lynz), lines on a topographic map that indicate areas with the same elevation, or height above sea level (C10)

convection (kuhn VEHK shuhn), transfer of thermal energy by the flow of liquids or gases (F89)

core (kohr), Earth's innermost structure (C41)

crust (kruhst), the thin, rocky outer layer of Earth that makes up the continents and the ocean floor (C7, C40)

density (DEHN sih tee), mass per unit volume of a substance (E44)

deposition (dehp uh ZIHSH uhn), [1] constructive force in which sediments that have been moved from one place are dropped or released in another place, or [2] change of state from a gas to a solid (C24, E86)

desert (DEHZ uhrt), a very dry area (B14)

diffusion (dih FYOO zhuhn), movement of particles from an area of higher concentration to an area of lower concentration (A17)

DNA molecule found in the nucleus of a cell and shaped like a double helix; associated with the transfer of genetic information (A86)

dome mountains (dohm MOWN tuhnz), mountains that form when magma pushes up on Earth's crust but does not break through (C64)

dominant trait (DAHM uh nuhnt trayt), trait that is expressed when an organism receives genes for two different forms of a trait (A99)

earthquake (URTH kwayk), violent shaking of Earth's crust as built-up energy is released (C54)

ecosystem (EHK oh sihs tuhm), all the living and nonliving things that interact with one another in a given area (B6)

El Niño (ehl NEE nyo), periodic change in the direction of warm ocean currents across the Pacific Ocean (D10)

electric cell (ih LEHK trihk sehl), device that uses a chemical reaction to produce electricity

electric circuit (ih LEHK trihk SUR kiht), pathway for an electric current (F112)

electric current (ih LEHK trihk KUR uhnt), continuous flow of electric charge along a pathway

electric generator (ih LEHK trihk JEHN uh ray tuhr), device that converts kinetic energy to electricity (F107)

electric motor (ih LEHK trihk MOH tuhr), device that converts electrical energy into kinetic energy (F126)

electromagnet (ih lehk troh MAG niht), a magnet that is powered by electricity (F32)

electron (ih LEHK trahn), a particle in an atom that has a negative charge (E7)

element (EHL uh muhnt), a substance that cannot be broken down into other substances (E6)

endangered species (ehn DAYN juhrd SPEE sheez), a species close to becoming extinct (B59)

energy (EHN uhr jee), ability to do work (F44)

epicenter (EHP ih sehn tuhr), point on Earth's surface directly above the focus of an earthquake (C54)

erosion (ih ROH zhuhn), destructive force in which pieces of rock are moved by water, wind, or moving ice (C16)

experiment (ihks SPEHR uh muhnt), to investigate and collect data that either supports a hypothesis or shows that it is false while controlling variables and changing only one part of an experimental setup at a time

extinction (ihk STIHNGK shuhn), when all members of a species die out (B51)

fault (fawlt), crack in Earth's crust along which movement takes place (C52)

fault-block mountains (fahwlt blahk MOWN tuhnz), mountains that form along fault lines where blocks of rock fall, are thrust up, or slide (C63)

flagellum (fluh JEHL uhm), whip-like tail that helps single-celled organisms move by spinning like a propeller (A17)

focus (FOH kuhs), point underground where the faulting in an earthquake occurs (C54)

fold mountains (fohld MOWN tuhnz), mountains that form where two plates collide and force layers of rock into folds (C62)

food chain (food chayn), description of how energy in an ecosystem flows from one organism to another (B25)

food web (food wehb), description of all the food chains in an ecosystem (B26)

force (fawrs), push or pull acting on an object (F7)

fossil (FAH suhl), physical remains or traces of a plant or animal that lived long ago (C44)

fossil fuel (FAHS uhl fyool), nonrenewable resource formed from ancient plants and animals (C75)

friction (FRIHK shuhn), force from rubbing (F12)

front (fruhnt), narrow region between two air masses that have different properties (D19)

fungi (FUHN jee), kingdom of living things; its organisms are multicellular, have nuclei, and often feed on decaying matter (A26)

galaxy (GAL uhk see), an enormous system of gases, dust, and stars held together by gravity (D78)

gas (gas), state of matter that has no definite shape or volume (E78)

gene (jeen), short segment of DNA that determines an organism's inherited traits (A87)

grasslands (GRAS landz), land covered by grasses with few trees (B14)

gravity (GRAV ih tee), pulling force between objects (F12)

gymnosperms (JIHM nuh spurmz), plants with seeds that are not covered by protective fruits (A69)

habitat (HAB ih tat), the natural environment where an organism lives (B38)

heat (heet), transfer of thermal energy from warmer areas to cooler areas (F80)

heredity (huh REHD ih tee), genetic transfer of characteristics from parent to offspring (A84)

hybrid (HY brihd), organism that has two different genes for the same trait (A99)

hypothesize (hy PAHTH uh syz), to make an educated guess about why something happens

inertia (ih NUR shuh), resistance to a change in motion (F7)

infer (ihn FUR), to use facts, data, and observations to draw a conclusion about a specific event

inner planets (IHN uhr PLAN ihtz), the four planets of the solar system that are closest to the sun — Mercury, Venus, Earth, and Mars (D64)

insulator (IHN suh lay tuhr), material that does not easily transfer thermal energy or electricity (F92)

invertebrate (ihn VUR tuh briht), animal that has no internal skeleton or bones (A28)

kinetic energy (kih NEHT ihk EHN uhr jee), energy of a moving object (F46)

kingdom (KIHNG duhm), largest group of organisms that share traits in common (A24)

life cycle (lyf SY kuhl), sequence of life events beginning with a seed and ending with the next generation of seeds (A68)

light-year (LYT yihr), unit of measurement for distances outside the solar system and equal to about 9.5 trillion km (D75)

liquid (LIHK wihd), state of matter that has a definite volume, but no definite shape (E77)

lithosphere (LIHTH uh sfihr), shell formed from Earth's solid upper mantle and crust (C41)

lunar eclipse (LOO nuhr ih KLIHPS), when Earth passes directly between the Sun and the Moon, casting a shadow on the Moon (D46)

magma (MAG muh), melted rock below Earth's surface; called lava at the surface (C56)

magnitude (MAG nih tood), brightness of a star as perceived from Earth (D75)

mantle (MAN tl), thick layer of Earth's structure just below Earth's crust (C41)

measure (MEHZH uhr), to use a variety of measuring instruments and tools to find the length, distance, volume, mass, or temperature using appropriate units of measurement

mechanical wave (mih KAN ih kuhl wayv), wave that can travel only through matter (F52)

melting (MEHL tihng), change of state from a solid to a liquid as energy is added (E84)

melting point (MEHL tihng point), temperature at which a substance changes from a solid to a liquid (E45)

mesosphere (MEHZ oh sfeer), layer of the atmosphere above the stratosphere and below the thermosphere (D17)

metal (MEHT l), any one of the elements located on the left and bottom of the periodic table, which are usually shiny, can be bent or stretched, and conduct electricity (E17)

meteor (MEE tee uhr), chunk of matter that enters Earth's atmosphere and is heated by friction with the air (D60)

meteorites (MEE tee uh rytz), chunks of meteor matter that fall to the ground (D60)

mixture (MIHKS chuhr), physical combination of two or more substances (E60)

molecule (MAHL ih kyool), two or more atoms joined by chemical bonds (E10)

moon phases (moon FAYZ ihz), shapes created by the changing amounts of the visible lighted areas of the Moon (D44)

motion (MOH shuhn), change in an object's position (F6)

mutation (myoo TAY shuhn), change in the genes of an organism (A89)

natural resource (NACH uhr uhl REE sawrs), resource found in nature, such as air, water, minerals, and soil (C74)

neutron (NOO trahn), a particle in the nucleus of an atom that has no charge (E8)

newton (NOOT n), unit to measure force, it is equal to the force required to accelerate a 1 kg mass by 1 m/s^2 (F11)

niche (nihch), the role of an organism in its habitat (B39)

noble gas (NOH buhl gas), any one of the elements located in the far right column of the periodic table, which generally do not combine with other elements to form molecules (E20)

nonmetal (nahn MEHT l), elements that are usually dull, brittle, and do not conduct electricity (E17)

nonrenewable resource (nahn rih NOO uh buhl REE sawrs), resource that is difficult to replace (C75)

nonvascular plant (nahn VAS kyoo luhr plant), a simple plant that lacks true leaves, stems, and roots (A62)

nucleotide (NOO klee uh tyd), basic structural unit of DNA (A87)

nucleus (NOO klee uhs), storehouse of the cell's most important chemical information, or the central core of an atom (A8, E7)

observe (UHB zuhrv), to use the senses and tools to gather or collect information and determine the properties of objects or events

ocean current (OH shuhn KUR uhnt), moving stream of water created by winds pushing against the ocean's surface (D10)

organ (AWR guhn), group of one or more kinds of tissues that work together to perform the same function (A33)

organ system (AWR guhn SIHS tuhm), group of interconnected organs that perform related life functions (A33)

organelle (AWR guh nehl), cell structure that performs specific functions (A8)

osmosis (ahz MOH sihs), type of diffusion in which water passes through a cell membrane (A17)

outer planets (OW tuhr PLAN ihtz), the four planets of the solar system farthest from the Sun—Jupiter, Saturn, Uranus, and Neptune (D66)

parallel circuit (PAR uh lehl SUR kiht), circuit where electric current can follow two or more different paths (F115)

penumbra (pih NUHM bruh), large partial shadow in an eclipse (D46)

periodic table (pihr ee AHD ihk   TAY buhl), a table that organizes the elements by their properties (E15)

phloem (FLOH ehm), specialized tissue within roots, stems, and leaves that moves materials (A63)

photosynthesis (foh toh SIHN thih sihs), the process by which plants use light energy to convert water and carbon dioxide into sugars and oxygen (A50)

physical change (FIHZ ih kuhl   chaynj), change in the size, shape, or state of matter with no new matter being formed (E52)

physical property (FIHZ ih kuhl   PRAHP uhr tee), characteristic that can be measured or detected by the senses (E43)

pitch (pihch), perceived highness or lowness of a sound (F56)

planet (PLAN iht), large bodies that revolve around the Sun (D56)

plate tectonics (playt   tehk TAHN ihks), theory that giant plates of crust are moving slowly across Earth's surface (C42)

pollination (pahl ih NAY shuhn), process of delivering pollen (male) to the egg (female) in a plant (A69)

pollution (puh LOO shuhn), addition of harmful substances to the environment (B60)

population (pahp yuh LAY shuhn), all the members of the same type of organism living in an ecosystem (B8, B46)

population density (pahp yuh LAY shuhn DEHN sih tee), number of individuals in a population in a given area (B47)

potential energy (puh TEHN shuhl   EHN uhr jee), energy stored in an object (F46)

predator (PREHD uh tuhr), animal that hunts and eats other animals (B47)

predict (prih DIHKT), to state what you think will happen based on past experience, observations, patterns, and cause-and-effect relationships

prey (pray), animal that is hunted and eaten by predators (B47)

producer (pruh DOO suhr), organism that makes its own food from raw materials and energy (B24)

protist (PROH tihst), kingdom of living things; its organisms are mostly one-celled but have nuclei and other organelles (A25)

proton (PROH tahn), a particle in the nucleus of an atom that has a positive charge (E8)

protostar (PROH tuh stahr), first stage in the formation of a star (D76)

radiation (ray dee AY shuhn), transfer of thermal energy through electromagnetic waves (F90)

recessive trait (rih SEHS ihv   trayt), trait that is not expressed when an organism receives genes for two different forms of a trait (A99)

record data (rih KAWRD   DAY tuh), to write, draw, audio record, video record, or photograph to show observations

recycling (ree SY klihng), process of recovering a resource from one item and using it to make another item (C92)

reflection (rih FLEHK shuhn), bouncing of a wave off a material (F66)

refraction (rih FRAK shuhn), changing of the path of a wave as it moves between materials of different densities (F66)

renewable resource (rih NOO uh buhl   REE sawrs), resource that is easily replaced or renewed (C76)

research (rih SURCH), to learn more about a subject by looking in books, newspapers, magazines, CD-ROMS, searching the Internet, or asking science experts

residual soil (rih ZIHJ oo uhl   soyl), soil formed directly from the bedrock below it (C85)

revolution (rehv uh LOO shuhn), one full trip, or orbit, around the Sun (D33)

S

scientific inquiry (sy uhn TIH fik IN kwih ree), method scientists use to ask and answer questions about the world around them (S3)

sediment (SEHD uh muhnt), small pieces of rock (C14)

seismic waves (SYZ mihk wayvz), waves of energy sent through Earth's crust when parts of the crust move suddenly (C53)

selective breeding (suh LEHK tihv BREE ding), practice of breeding plants and animals for desirable traits (A100)

semi-metal (SEHM ee meht l), elements that have some properties of metals and some properties of nonmetals (E17)

series circuit (SIHR eez SUR kiht), circuit where only a single path for electricity connects two or more devices (F114)

sexual reproduction (SEHK shoo uhl ree pruh DUHK shuhn), production of offspring by the union of male and female gametes (A98)

simple machine (SIHM puhl muh SHEEN), a machine that has few or no moving parts (F17)

soil (soyl), natural resource made up of small rocks, minerals, water, gases, and organic matter (C84)

soil profile (soyl PROH fyl), all of the soil horizons, or layers, in a soil sample (C86)

solar eclipse (SOH luhr ih KLIHPS), when the Moon passes directly between the Sun and Earth, casting a shadow on Earth (D46)

solar system (SOH luhr SIHS tuhm), the Sun and all bodies that revolve around it (D56)

solid (SAHL ihd), state of matter that has a definite shape and volume (E76)

solubility (sahl yuh BIHL ih tee), measure of how much of one substance can dissolve in another substance (E46)

solute (SAHL yoot), substance that is dissolved in a solution (E62)

solution (suh LOO shuhn), mixture of two or more substances that are evenly distributed throughout the mixture (E62)

solvent (SAHL vuhnt), substance that dissolves the solute in a solution (E62)

speed (speed), measure of the distance an object moves in a given unit of time (F8)

spores (spawrz), reproductive structures found in fungi and simple plants (A68)

stars (stahrz), giant sphere of glowing gases (D74)

state of matter (stayt uhv MAT uhr), physical form that matter takes; gas, liquid, and solid (E74)

static electricity (STAT ihk ih lehk TRIHS ih tee), electrical force between nonmoving electric charges (F104)

stomata (STOH muh tuh), small openings through which gases move in and out of leaves (A52)

stratosphere (STRA tuh sfeer), layer of the atmosphere above the troposphere and below the mesosphere (D17)

sublimation (suhb luh MAY shuhn), change of state from a solid to a gas (E86)

subsoil (SUHB soyl), layer of soil beneath the topsoil (C86)

summer solstice (SUHM uhr SAHL stihs), June 21 or 22, the longest day of the year in the Northern Hemisphere (D34)

switch (swihch), movable section of a circuit that can open or close a path for electricity (F113)

symbiosis (sihm bee OH sihs), close, long-lasting relationship between species (B42)

T

taiga (TY guh), area that has long, severe winters and short, cool summers (B15)

technology (tehk NAH luh jee), tools, things built with tools, or methods used to accomplish a practical purpose (S11)

temperate forests forests that experience four distinct seasons: summer, fall, winter, and spring (B13)

temperature (TEHM puhr uh chur), measure of the average kinetic energy of the particles that make up a substance (F78)

thermal energy total kinetic energy of the particles of a substance (F78)

thermal expansion (THUHR muhl ihk SPAN shuhn), increase in size of a substance due to a change in temperature (E87)

thermosphere (THUHR muh sfeer), the outermost layer of the atmosphere, above the mesosphere (D17)

threatened species (THREHT nd SPEE sheez), a species close to becoming endangered (B59)

tissue (TIHSH oo), group of one or more kinds of specialized cells that perform the same function (A33)

topographic map map that shows the shape of surface features and their elevations above sea level (C10)

topsoil uppermost layer of soil (C86)

transpiration (tran spuh RAY shuhn), evaporation through the leaves of a plant (A64)

transported soil (trans PAWRT ihd soyl), soil that has been carried from one place to another by erosion (C85)

tropical rain forests forests in regions that are very hot and very rainy (B13)

troposphere (TROH puh sfihr), layer of Earth's atmosphere closest to Earth's surface and containing about three-quarters of the atmosphere's gases (D17)

tundra Earth's coldest biome (B15)

umbra (UHM bruh), small, dark shadow in an eclipse (D46)

use variables (yooz VAIR ee uh buhlz), to keep all conditions in an experiment the same except for the variable, or the condition that is being tested

vaporization (vay puh rih ZAY shuhn), change of state from a liquid to a gas as energy is added (E85)

vascular plant a plant with specialized tissues and organs for transporting materials (A63)

velocity (vuh LAHS ih tee), measure of speed and direction (F8)

vernal equinox (VUR nuhl EE kwuh nahks), March 20 or 21, when the number of hours of daylight and darkness are the same (D34)

vertebrate (VUR tuh briht), animal that has an internal skeleton or backbone (A26)

vibration (vy BRAY shuhn), rapid back-and-forth movement (F54)

visible light portion of the electro-magnetic spectrum humans can see (F65)

voltage (VOHL tihj), measure of the force that moves electrons (F127)

volume (VAHL yoom), loudness of a sound, or the space an object takes up (F57)

weathering destructive force that breaks down rocks into smaller pieces (C14)

winter solstice (WIHN tuhr SAHL stihs), December 21 or 22, the shortest day of the year in the Northern Hemisphere (D34)

work (wurk), result of a force moving an object a certain distance (F16)

xylem (ZY luhm), specialized plant tissue that moves materials (A63)

Index

Index

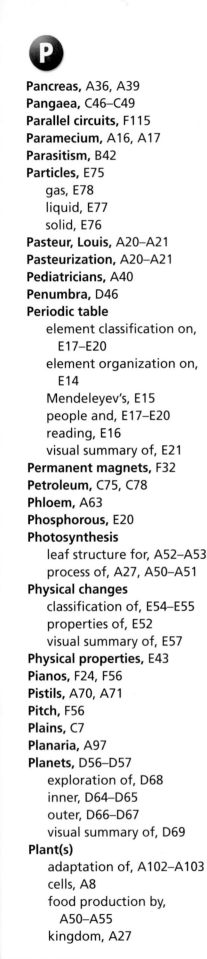

Index

Index

Literature:

Excerpt from *The River of Grass* from *Everglades: Buffalo Tiger and the River of Grass,* by Peter Lourie. Copyright © 1994 by Peter Lourie. Reprinted by permission of Caroline House, Boyds Mills Press, Inc.

Some Rivers from *Sawgrass Poems: A View From the Everglades.* Copyright © 1996 by Frank Asch. Reprinted by permission of Harcourt, Inc. This material may not be reproduced in any form or by any means without the prior written permission of the publisher.

Excerpt from *Salt Marshes and Protector of Land and Animals* from *The Florida Water Story: From Raindrops to the Sea,* by Peggy Sias Lantz and Wendy A. Hale. Copyright © 1998 by Peggy Sias Lantz and Wendy A. Hale. Reprinted by permission of Pineapple Press, Inc.

Excerpt from *Comets, Meteors, and Asteroids,* by Seymour Simon. Copyright © 1994 by Seymour Simon. Reprinted by permission of William Morrow and Company, an imprint of HarperCollins Publishers.

Earth Changed in Meteor's Fiery Death from *Earth Shake: Poems From the Ground Up,* by Lisa Westberg Peters, Illustrated by Cathie Felstead. Text copyright © 2003 by Lisa Westberg Peters, illustrations copyright 2003 by Cathie Felstead. Reprinted by permission of Harper-Collins Publishers.

Photography:

Front and back cover (tiger) © Joe McDonald/Corbis. (front cover bkgd) © Randy Wells/Corbis. **Spine** © PhotoDisc, Inc./Getty Images. **Page iv** © Mark Tomalty/Masterfile Stock Photo Library. **v** © Corbis/Punch Stock. **vi** © William Manning/Corbis. **vii** Courtesy of NASA. **viii** © Dorling Kindersley Picture Library. **ix** © Fukuhara, Inc./Corbis. **ix** © Fukuhara, Inc./Corbis. **S1** © LB Goodman/Omni-Photo Communications. **S2** Courtesy of Dr. Dale Brown Emeagwali. **S2-3** © Microfield Scientific Ltd./Photo Researchers, Inc. **S3** (r) © Alamy Images. **S4-5** (bkgd) © Picimpact/Corbis. Ocelot © Pete Oxford/Nature Picture Library. **S6** (bkgd) © Marc Muench/Muench Photography, Inc. **S9** (bkgd) © HMCo. **S10** (b) © Cassandra Wagner. **S10** (t) © Mitsuhiko Imamori/Minden Pictures. **S11** © Janet Hostetter/AP/Wide World Photos. **S12-13** (b) © Brand X Pictures/Punch Stock. **S12-13** (bkgd) © PhotoDisc, Inc./Punch Stock. **S14** © Stephen Frink/Corbis. **Unit A Opener pages** © Spike Walker/Getty Images. **A2-3** © David McCarthy/Science Photo Library/Photo Researchers, Inc. **A3** (1) © Leonard Lessin/Peter Arnold, Inc. **A3** (2) © VVG/Science Photo Library/Photo Researchers, Inc. **A3** (3) © Edward AM Snijde/Lonely Planet. **A3** (4) © Ariel Skelley/Corbis. **A4-5** © Mitsuaki Iwago/Minden Pictures. **A6** (l) © Omikron/Photo Researchers, Inc. **A6** (r) © The Granger Collection, New York. **A7** (b) © Dennis Kunkel Microscopy, Inc. **A7** (t) © Mark Tomalty/Masterfile Stock Photo Library. **A8** © Andrew Syred/Science Photo Library/Photo Researchers, Inc. **A9** © Dr. Gopal Murti/Photo Researchers, Inc. **A10** (b) © CNRI/Science Photo Library/Photo Researchers, Inc. **A10** (c) © Professors P. Motta & T. Naguro/Science Photo Library/Photo Researchers, Inc. **A10** (t) © Dr. Jeremy Burgess/Science Photo Library/Photo Researchers, Inc. **A11** (1) © Omikron/Photo Researchers, Inc. **A11** (2) © Leonard Lessin/Peter Arnold, Inc. **A11** (3) © Dr. Gopal Murti/Photo Researchers, Inc. **A11** (4) © Andrew Syred/Science Photo Library/Photo Researchers, Inc. **A12** © VVG/Science Photo Library/Photo

Researchers, Inc. **A12- 13** © Brandon D. Cole/Corbis. **A14** © WG/Science Photo Library/Photo Researchers, Inc. **A15** (b) © Science Photo Library/Photo Researchers, Inc. **A15** (t) © SciMAT/Photo Researchers, Inc. **A16** (b) © Andrew Syred/Science Photo Library/Photo Researchers, Inc. **A16** (t) © Melba Photo Agency/Alamy **A17** © Andrew Syred/Science Photo Library/Photo Researchers, Inc. **A18** © Andrew Syred/Photo Researchers, Inc. **A19** (b) © Andrew Syred/Photo Researchers, Inc. **A19** (c) © Andrew Syred/Science Photo Library/Photo Researchers, Inc. **A19** (t) © SciMAT/Photo Researchers, Inc. **A19** © SciMAT/Photo Researchers, Inc. **A20** (b) © The Granger Collection, New York. **A20** (t) © Popperfoto/Alamy Images. **A21** (b) © Index Stock Imagery, Inc. **A21** (t) © Larry Lefever/Grant Heilman Photography. **A22** © Digital Vision/Punch Stock. **A22-23** (bkgd) © Ian Cartwright/PhotoDisc, Inc./Getty Images. **A23** (c) © PhotoDisc, Inc. **A23** (l) © PhotoDisc, Inc. **A23** (r) © PhotoDisc, Inc. **A24** © Duncan Usher/Foto Natura/Minden Pictures. **A25** (1) © SciMAT/Photo Researchers, Inc. **A25** (2) © WG/Science Photo Library/Photo Researchers, Inc. **A25** (3) © RO-MA Stock/Index Stock Imagery. **A25** (4) © Goodshoot/Punch Stock. **A25** (5) © Corbis/Punch Stock. **A26** (b) © Corbis/Punch Stock. **A26** (t) © Kim Taylor and Jane Burton/Dorling Kindersley Picture Library. **A27** (b) © Nick Garbutt/Nature Picture Library. **A27** (t) © Peter Johnson/Corbis. **A28** (b) © Gary Bell/Getty Images. **A28** (t) © Dave Roberts/Science Photo Library/Photo Researchers, Inc. **A30-31** © A. Syred/Photo Researchers, Inc. **A32** © Innerspace Imaging/Photo Researchers, Inc. **A35** (b) © Jerry Young/Dorling Kindersley Picture Library. **A35** (t) © Ron Boardman; Frank Lane Picture Agency/Corbis. **A38** © Chris Hellier/Corbis. **A40** © Ariel Skelley/Corbis. **A42-43** © Steve Gschmeissner/Science Photo Library/Photo Researchers, Inc. **A45** (l) © SciMAT/Photo Researchers, Inc. **A45** © Andrew Syred/Science Photo Library/Photo Researchers, Inc. **A46-47** © Steve Hopkin/Getty Images. **A47** (b) Paul McCormick/The Image Bank/Getty Images. **A47** (c) © Eduardo Garcia/Taxi/Getty Images. **A47** (t) © Barry Runk/Stan/Grant Heilman Photography, Inc. **A48-49** © Medford Taylor/National Geographic Society. **A50** © Wesley Hitt/Mira.com. **A51** © Barry Runk/Stan/Grant Heilman Photography, Inc. **A52** © Runk/Shoenberger/Grant Heilman Photography, Inc. **A52** (r) © Runk/Shoenberger/Grant Heilman Photography, Inc. **A53** (b) © Andrew Syred/Science Photo Library/Photo Researchers, Inc. **A54** © Claus Meyer/Minden Pictures. **A55** (b) © Claus Meyer/Minden Pictures. **A55** (t) © Wesley Hitt/Mira.com. **A57** (l) © PhotoDisc, Inc./Punch Stock. **A57** (r) © Inga Spence/IndexStock. **A58** (1) © Biosphoto/Peter Arnold Inc. **A58** (2) © Norbert Wu/Peter Arnold, Inc. **A58** (3) © Ed Reschke/Peter Arnold, Inc. **A58** (4) © Inga Spence/Alamy. **A59** (b) © The Granger Collection, New York. **A59** (t inset) © Patrick Johns/Corbis. **A59** (tr) © Mario Tama/Getty Images. **A60-61** Peter Marbach/Grant Heilman Photography, Inc. **A62** (l) © Richard Cummins/Corbis. **A62** (r) © Dr. Jeremy Burgess/Photo Researchers, Inc. **A63** (b) © Alfred Pasieka/Science Photo Library/Photo Researchers, Inc. **A63** (t) © Sheila Terry/Science Photo Library/Photo Researchers, Inc. **A65** (c) © Alfred Pasieka/Science Photo Library/Photo Researchers, Inc. **A65** (t) © Richard Cummins/Corbis. **A66** © Ed Degginger/Bruce Coleman, Inc. **A66-67** © Digital Vision/Punch Stock. **A68** © David Forster/Alamy **A69** (b) © blickwinkel/Alamy. **A69** (r) © James Morgan/Dorling

Kindersley Picture Library. **A69** (br) © Rich Reid/National Geographic/Getty Images. **A72** (b) © Dwight Kuhn/Bruce Coleman, Inc. **A72** (t) © Peter Steyn/Photo Access/Taxi/Getty Images. **A73** (bl) © Georgette Douwma/The Image Bank/Getty Images. **A73** (br) © Steve Maslowski/Photo Researchers, Inc. **A73** (t) © Lynn Ponto-Peterson. **A74** (bl) © Inga Spence/IndexStock. **A74** (br) © Davies & Starr/Stone/Getty Images. **A74** (cl) © Mark Tomalty/Masterfile Stock Photo Library. **A74** (cr) © Rick Souders/Food Pix. **A74** (tl) © Dwight Kuhn. **A74** (tr) © Lois Ellen Frank/Corbis. **A76-77** © Dr. Jeremy Burgess/Science Photo Library/Photo Researchers, Inc. **A76** (c) © Claude Nuridsany & Marie Perennou/Science Photo Library/Photo Researchers, Inc. **A80-81** © Allen Russell/Index Stock Imagery. **A81** (b) © George Grall/National Geographic Image Collection **A81** (t) © Rod Williams/Nature Picture Library. **A82** © Paul Eekhoff/Masterfile Stock Photo Library. **A82-83** © ImageState/Alamy Images Ltd. **A84** © Robert Stock **A85** (b) © Rod Williams/Nature Picture Library. **A85** (t) © Buzz Pictures/Alamy Images. **A86** © Carolina Biological Supply Company/PhotoTake USA. **A89** (inset) © Kaj R. Svenson/Science Photo Library/Photo Researchers, Inc. **A89** © PhotoDisc, Inc. **A90** © Eye of Science/Photo Researchers, Inc. **A91** (b) © Kaj R. Svenson/Science Photo Library/Photo Researchers, Inc. **A91** (t) © Rod Williams/Nature Picture Library. **A92** (b) © Omikron/Photo Researchers, Inc. **A92** (t) © Photo Researchers, Inc. **A93** © Luis Rico **A94** © Yva Momatiuk/John Eastcott/Minden Pictures. **A94-95** © Prenzel, Fritz/Earth Scenes. **A96** (inset) © Melba Photo Agency/Alamy. **A97** (b) © Dennis Kunkel Microscopy, Inc. **A97** (t) © Andrew J. Martinez/Photo Researchers, Inc. **A99** (l) © Corel/FotoSearch. **A99** (r) © Ulf Wallin/The Image Bank/Getty Images. **A100** (c) © Davies & Starr/The Image Bank/Getty Images. **A100** (l) © Brand X Pictures/Punch Stock. **A100** (r) © Ed Young/Corbis. **A101** (l) © Peter Cade/Stone/Getty Images. **A101** (r) © PhotoDisc, Inc./Punch Stock. **A102** (bl) © Ruth Cole, Animals Animals. **A102** (br) © Peter Blackwell/Nature Picture Library. **A102** (t) © Jeffrey L. Rotman/Peter Arnold, Inc. **A103** (c) © Zigmund Leszczynski/Animals Animals. **A103** (l) © Mark Moffett/Minden Pictures. **A103** (r) © David M. Dennis/Animals Animals- Earth Scenes. **A104** (b) © Melba Photo Agency/Alamy. **A104** (c) © Peter Cade/Stone/Getty Images. **A104** (t) © David M. Dennis/Animals Animals- Earth Scenes. **A105** (t) © Jim Whitmer. **A105** (b) © Patrick Olear/PhotoEdit, Inc. **A106** © Stephen Green-Armytage. **Unit B Opener first page** ©Tom and Pat Leeson. **Unit B Opener spread** ©Gary Kramer. **B2-3** © Kevin Schafer Photography. **B3** (b) © Dwight Kuhn. **B3** (c) © David Mendelsohn/Masterfile Stock Photo Library. **B3** (t) © Dwight Kuhn. **B4** © George McCarthy/Corbis. **B4-5** © Gary Braasch/Corbis. **B6** © Mark Barrett/Index Stock Imagery. **B6-7** (bkgd) © David Muench/Corbis. **B7** (c) © Jeff Lepore/Photo Researchers, Inc. **B7** (l) © Frans Lanting/Minden Pictures. **B7** (r) © Dwight Kuhn Photography. **B8** © Alexis Rosenfeld/Photo Researchers, Inc. **B9** (b) © Alexis Rosenfeld/Photo Researchers, Inc. **B9** (c) © Dwight Kuhn Photography. **B9** (t) © Mark Barrett/Index Stock Imagery. **B10** © W. Perry Conway/Corbis. **B10-11** © National Geographic Society. **B13** (b) © Darrell Gulin/Corbis. **B13** (deer) © Stephen J. Krasemann/Photo Researchers, Inc. **B13** (t) © Kevin Schafer Photography. **B13** (toucan) © Cyril Laubscher/Dorling Kindersley Picture Library. **B14** (b) © Corbis/Punch Stock. **B14** (gila) © Jerry Young/Dorling Kindersley Photo